WALKING
GENTRY
HOME

WALKING GENTRY HOME

A Memoir of My Foremothers in Verse

ALORA YOUNG

HOGARTH

London/New York

Published in the United States by Hogarth, an imprint of Random House, a division of Penguin Random House LLC, New York.

HOGARTH is a trademark of the Random House Group Limited, and the H colophon is a trademark of Penguin Random House LLC.

LIBRARY OF CONGRESS CATALOGING-IN-PUBLICATION DATA
Names: Young, Alora, author.
Title: Walking Gentry home : a memoir of my foremothers in verse / Alora Young.
Description: London ; New York : Hogarth, [2022] |
Identifiers: LCCN 2021058451 (print) | LCCN 2021058452 (ebook) | ISBN 9780593498002 (trade paperback) | ISBN 9780593498019 (ebook)
Subjects: LCSH: Young, Alora—Family—Poetry. | African American girls—Poetry. | African American women—Poetry. | Halls (Tenn.)—History—Poetry. | LCGFT: Autobiographical poetry. | Young adult nonfiction.
Classification: LCC PS3625.O933 W35 2022 (print) | LCC PS3625.O933 (ebook) | DDC 811/.6—dc23/eng/20211215
LC record available at https://lccn.loc.gov/2021058451
LC ebook record available at https://lccn.loc.gov/2021058452

Printed in Canada on acid-free paper

randomhousebooks.com

9 8 7 6 5 4 3 2 1

First Edition

Book design by Caroline Cunningham

For Gentry,

and every girl who needs somebody to walk with

CONTENTS

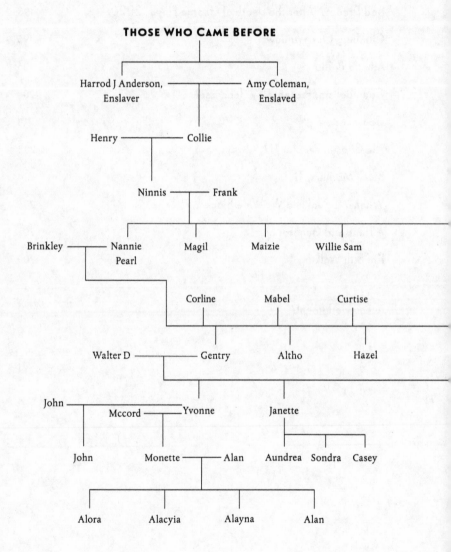

THOSE WHO CAME BEFORE

Harrod J Anderson, Enslaver ———— Amy Coleman, Enslaved

Henry ———— Collie

Ninnis ———— Frank

Brinkley ———— Nannie Pearl   Magil   Maizie   Willie Sam

Corline   Mabel   Curtise

Walter D ———— Gentry   Altho   Hazel

John ———— Mccord ———— Yvonne   Janette

John   Monette ———— Alan   Aundrea   Sondra   Casey

Alora   Alacyia   Alayna   Alan

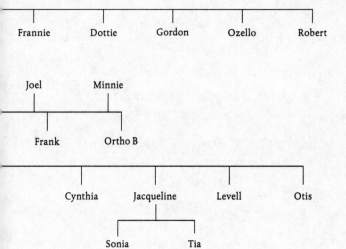

Frannie   Dottie   Gordon   Ozello   Robert

Joel   Minnie

Frank   Ortho B

Cynthia   Jacqueline   Levell   Otis

Sonia   Tia

WALKING FOREWORD

THIS HOME OF MINE LIES in the steam that rolls off the hot water cornbread. It is singed fingertips from tinfoil-wrapped fried bologna sandwiches. It is tiptoeing barefoot to the ice cream truck over old sienna pavement. It is the best Dollar General on either side of the Mississippi. My home is the one-to-one pickup-truck-to-people ratio; everyone in this town has their all-wheel-drive alter ego. My home is in the honey mustard that sticks to the lid of the to-go packets that come with Exxon fried chicken. In my home even the gnats move slow, just taking their time. You can see the heat if you look hard enough. It leaves you sweating like a sinner in the Lord's house. My home has a patina like a skillet of cast iron, a thousand times seasoned, a million times fired. My home is a tiny town in West Tennessee that for centuries you could barely find on a map. I carry it with me always.

Halls is the town where my mothers have lived since their beginning in this country. The kind of place where everyone is family. It's where I found God, the second time. It's the place that taught me love is unconditional and unrelenting. The people I love that thrived there die with the changing seasons. I watch the thrift shops and candy stores get boarded up and fade into phantoms of their former selves. I have been shaped by the way towns die because it taught me legacies can be forever. I wonder if it's healthy to love a thing that's as good as dead.

In Halls, I am the bearer of a prophecy. From the moment Momma's body opened, they said I was the one they waited for. They say I'm the culmination of a thousand generations of brilliant women, prayers, internal warfare, deferred dreams. They have told me I am every voice and poem that never graced a page, or another's ears and eyes. And because I bear this prophecy, I think it's my fault every time one of their dreams dies.

This multigenerational memoir in verse chronicles the lineage of a group of Black women and girls in West Tennessee, from unrecorded history to the 1700s up to my life in the present day. These are not just any girls, however; they are my foremothers. In the beginning, we have a series of poems about my ancestors whose names we no longer know, before arriving at my several-greats-grandmother Collie, the child of an enslaved woman and her enslaver in the days when Tennessee was still primarily wilderness. We follow a teenage Gentry, my great-grandmother, as she moves out of her mother's home to marry at fourteen; my grandmother when she had my mother at seventeen; my mother, the beauty queen; and finally, we come to the present day, with me, attempting to recover the legacy of the then-teenage girls whose lives of hard work and limited opportunity led to the now-teenage me writing their long-forgotten history.

The only way to tell this story is through poetry, because Black girlhood is eternally laced with rhythm, from the Negro hymns Amy Coleman whispered as she bore her enslaver's child to the rhythm of the gospel my mother sang at fifteen when she was hailed a child prodigy.

Walking Gentry Home is a story about girlhood and how the world scoffs at the way Black women come of age. It is an American story that persists, and we persist in ignoring it. The innocence and adolescence of Black girls are stories that are desperately needed because Black girls begin being called women far before they know what women really are.

This is for them—and for me.

Numbers

Alora, daughter of Monette, daughter of Yvonne, daughter of Gentry, daughter of Nannie Pearl, daughter of Ninnis, daughter of Collie, daughter of Amy, daughter of unknown, unknown, unknown

PART ONE

THE STORY BEFORE:
I AM BECAUSE YOU ARE

Prehistory–1865

Mothers, TN, Many Many Generations

I have many mothers
They are mostly Black
They are mostly broken
They have existed here for centuries
They are dying with the towns that birthed them

Show Me the Company You Keep I'll Tell You Who You Are, Part I

My favorite company has always been that of ghosts.
Hear me out,
I mean that I find the most comfort surrounded by stories
    from the past.
People from the past.

Worlds that have faded into hills or cityscapes.
This is a story about girlhood,
and artists,
and a town in West Tennessee that keeps on dying.
I suppose I tell it because when you find
so much comfort in dead things,
you know the worst part
is that they are only alive in your head.
My family's story is possibly yours too.
Because even when eras change,
girls will inevitably grow up
and fall in love and bleed
and fall out of love and fight over blood,
and my god will they fight over it.
Adolescence,
more specifically girlhood, is a bloodbath.
My mom has a habit of telling me things
I'm not yet sure I'm ready to believe.
Recently she has been telling me

this world is ready for me to be a woman.
Giving up being a girl
is more terrifying
than Halls dying
so I'm trying to save this
aging place because my favorite
girls/ghosts
all lurk there.
Perhaps this is just me running
away from one more dying thing.

A Lot See But a Few Know. Halls, TN. Always.

It's a funny thing being born.

Someone
carried us for about nine months
and that one person
will always know
where we came from.
Them.
But that's where things start to get complicated;
it gets blurry as we get less concentrated;
we zoom out on the camera of history
and like the smallest part of cells
the microscopic organelles
once you zoom far enough
they just disappear.
But they're still here,
we're still here.
My story goes back centuries
but I see so few generations

my culture is calamity
and far away nations
my blood bleeds into endless cotton fields
of empty stalks on family trees.
My ancestry was lost
in chains and boats across the seas.

Am I aristocracy?
Do I belong to a great nation?
What if my Black Girl Magic
is just cultural appropriation?
My genes are on a selfish streak
and decided to abstain

from sharing what runs in my veins
with my desperate brain.
I never know if my identity

is more than just a guise
all I have to go off
is a fro and slanted eyes.
My recipe remains a mystery
and as I grow and die
I crave any bit of history that takes the question
    out of I.
I want the glittery grains of broken past
that cut me deep like broken glass
to hold tightly in my hand
but the powerful don't care

for it's their world that we must understand.
We are all dying and degrading
every second till we're dead
from the moment we're born

—

to exist in our heads.
Like history melting into the ground that we tread
the only stories that survive are the ones we've all read
but the only ones I want to hear are the ones we left unsaid.

1765 the start of a revolution

Phillis Wheatley slung syllables
and sent her slavers absolution.

But she fades to the grind of time
to the Bible of brilliant Black women
with its withering spine.

We neglect to remember an astonishing mind
because her symphonic synapses
sulked beyond sepia skin.
Who am I but a fiber in the hive mind of history?
Praying for a fighting chance
to outwit the sophistry
that the victors imbued

every textbook with.
I wish to untwist the thread
every fact from myth
but no matter how hard I try
my textbooks lack melanin.
If not a slave then a felon and

I can't find my future
if I don't know my past.
I am a Black woman
as the standardized test said
but who knows if my genes
bleed black, white, or red.
I talk about melanin
but I haven't much to spare;
the only strand that ties me to my people
lies in the coils of my hair.
How do I identify when my blood is an enigma?
My pigment is more akin to unbleached paper.
I cried the day my white best friend
came home from vacation
and she was darker than me.
That year I swore
every Halloween
to go as a strong Black woman from history.
And I did
from C. J. to Colvin
through my mismatched shades
I was truly emboldened
and unafraid
cause we all remember Rosa
but we forget Claudette
and I wanted to make a change.
In the corner of my mind
I felt if others remembered

—

God would tell me who I was in exchange.
I know more about the world
than what's beneath my own skin.
It's easier to look out
than comprehend what's within.

Mitochondrial Eve, Africa, 150,000 Years Ago

My body is one hundred thousand years old.
It belonged to my momma
And to yours.
This body began back home.

I am afraid to call it the motherland
Because I am afraid to become a mother.
The Garden of Eden is lost to time
But it is in my DNA.
How strange
Were the fruits that God bore.

I believe that my body is infinite
Because God loves like a Black momma.

Strict
But strong
And true.

I believe that God made the universe
And I believe it hurt
And I believe that children tear from their mothers' bodies
With a pain like the labor of a star
So we know we are more than just
God's image.

When They Took Us, Benin and Togo, Circa 1560

The devil ripped right through my home like the troops
    marched to the sea.
The Atlantic had a reddened tide like the life that flows
    through me. The bloody ground bore fruit and now my
    country 'tis of thee.
Before the devil went down to Georgia he stopped by West
    Tennessee.
When he came Grandmama said God will handle everything.
    She tells me if she says a hen dips snuff, to peek beneath her
    wing.
If only Grandmama saw what had become of her hometown
The slaver's land that they had owned returned no longer free
In debt to the same twisted age of history.
Taken from the promised land
And the land promised to me.

Black Tax, America, 1650–Present

Every ancestor past was blast from traction
Every sin was burned into their umber skin
In the past, the anti-Black was common faction
Now they call it names of different kin.
But same facts.
Same acts.
The system stays though Crow is dead and over
Victimhood she claims another soldier
The wall is just a pit when you get over
Heartbeat like the gun that begs to smolder
My Africa is lost to ever after
My God rests in the tongue of slave master
The babies only know the name of bastard.
After all the hurt you give, the work we did
You can't stand to let us live
After mothers prayed we came out yellow bright

Cause cultures called "blind to color" in their spite
Still see different shades of Black and white.
And classists coddle fascists
While they fight that bullets bathed in blue
Need oversight.
They play that they don't see the way
the system stacks.

—

Can't bear to watch more Black men fall
through the cracks.
Black tax.

So go on and blame the Black blame the Black.
The heartland calls the blood but we resist.
We can only thank our chained-down wrist.
And when my zion comes they still persist.

Caucasian made the opioid a health crisis
When white men suffer sinful shifts to crimeless
Addict comes to culprit cause browns indicted
Spineless shoot our growth through the endocrine
This
Is how they make sure we do our time
For the misdemeanor of having too much melanin
Whole nation with a noose round our development
Black names equate with lack of eloquence
It's evident in all our hesitance
That relevance has precedence in only those considered to be
    Aryan.
Each defense you made displayed as an attack
But when you show 'em love they still blame the Black
Cuz their ingrained oppressions dressed up as a preference
When white is praised the brown girls learn a lesson
Love is not for you.
Anathema the music of the Congo
The culture lauds the bass before the bongo

Twice the work half all reward
Balance rests in the palm of a
White man's Lord
So go on and

Blame the Black blame the Black.
Soliloquy and Negro hymns raise palms and facts.

We match funerals and jumpsuits.
While they match attacks.

We watch women practice fourth-wave white feminism
And can't see past this, their own egotism
Twenty-nine cents is what's causing them strife
While we out here fighting twenty-five to life
Cause the war on drugs is the war on thugs
Is the war on Black brother by blue.
Same fight new time
Commonplace war crime
We're killing each other for you.
We come out the womb
Set to presume that the totalitarian
Booked a prison room
Cause every brown child's cradle
Is shaped like a tomb,
Tomb.
Someone to ostracize or privatize
Is the only thing that saves us from genocide

No one ever wept when a workhorse cried
White supremacy slept while Sandra died.

Just gonna blame the Black blame the Blacks.
Our stolen bodies don't come with contracts.

You'll never see what's happening here—
But if I'm angry and hate you nothing's gonna change
And my silence won't show you the ways people estrange
There's no way of rising if we try to climb alone
Hate burns and overtakes you
It destroys every home
You've gotta step up till bullets force you back
Cause if we burn down each other we'll all turn up Black
We gotta call out impunities, get guns off our blocks
Good schools in all communities and cameras on cops
And listen to each other.
We can work as one nation
Because I know for sure
Ignorance is born of isolation.
Unearthing every person underneath the privilege
We'll work with all the poison that the world has given
And soon Black will exist as culture, not as face
And we will only know this as the
Human race
And children down the line will solely know
Embrace
Brown girls in latter days won't need to learn that lesson

And character will be the only one contention
I don't have a dream, sisters I have a vision.
I don't have a dream, brothers I have a vision.
I don't have a dream
I have a vision.

This Country 1776

Halls is what America thinks it is.
When Yvonne died there KKK members came to grieve her.
Despite the battles that had to happen
white and Black people live there together.
They may be poor or dim but you love them all the while.
Halls is the kind of place that forces you to acknowledge your
   truth.
There is nowhere to hide in these four square miles.

Widows, Haywood County, 1790

I know two of my mothers
I know they were slaves
One was left in a will
Like an old dog
Or a set of china

Or a Negro I guess
I can't read about what
They did to the enslaved anymore
I just think about the pain my mothers
Took to their graves
I wonder if they peered into the eyes
Of the children
That garnered their freedom
And saw the men that sired them
I wonder what they would think
If they looked at me
If they would recognize
What became of their progeny
I don't know if these women
Were truly widows
But I suppose other truths

May not come as easily

Amy 1796

Amy was born nameless in Virginia

among the earliest generations
of slaves born into the new world.
When Harrod J Anderson set out to claim
a plot of land in the Mississippi river basin
Amy was taken
along with him.
She made the five-hundred-something-odd-mile journey

to Haywood County, Tennessee.
To wilderness
that sprouted into blood-watered fields of cotton.
Slavery and girlhood
were not mutually exclusive.
Collie, Amy's daughter,

lived on the same plot of land as her siblings and father,
yet she was owned by them.
She was said to have fair skin,
and supposedly her father
cared for her better than the others.
There was no double Dutch.
Amy taught Collie to cook well
and sew well
and care for her siblings,

both Black and white.
She said, "Baby, fear not,
for one day, we'll be free."
One. day.
The day of freedom that lurked in the Negro hymns.
Today

I only see Harrod J's tombstone carved of marble
that rises six feet high above the ground,
and Amy's, which does not exist.

Collie, b. 1837

Collie and Henry
were distant from what the traditions
of Black folks past indicated.
They were married.
And they were free.
Collie was born to a slaver and Amy,
her momma, enslaved the same.
She was light-skinned,
with light eyes, and she worked in the house.
Without a doubt,
her enslaver was her father.
And in secret, he treated her kindly.
He set her free between the pages of his will and yet still,
he was the man who had taken her mother so far away from
    the place of her birth.
He dragged her to an untamed world
in the hopes that he could make it into money.
I wonder if Collie ever looked
at her skin like I do and thought
about how it was the color of abuse.
How her body was made
in a mulatto shade
that made it known,
that she was not made with love but of suffering.
I wonder if she cared
for her white siblings in the house,

and watched her Black ones out in the field.
If the window was enough to separate her from the pain
she knew they would feel.
I wonder if she married Henry
because his color was enough
to hide, hide, hide
that history.

Becoming a Free Woman Haywood County Circa 1840

After Maya Angelou's "Caged Bird"

I know the world's dark now but
one day the sun will come out, a
society never thrives when it is Caged
like the one thing that never sings when it's aged, bird
at the edge of the cliff to freedom it stands
the world of old reality slips from her hands she moves on
and she finds a way to save the
only home she's ever known from the edge of the Grave
and she finds that her reality is not made of what it seems
and she learns to love again to spite his dreams
and she sees the world for real now she makes it hers
and out of the darkness, she sheds her shadow
and in the light, her heart starts to grow, she shouts,
"now that I am free I can finally go on"
"and into the daytime, I now glow on a
silly thing now can't dim my dream, no nightmare"
out of the dark world, she lets out a joyful scream

Dance On

I am from five generations of shotgun weddings
Of women with stronger wombs than wits

Of colorstruck
And dark skin
And wading into the forest to scrounge the ground for morels
    and morals
And damp earth to dance on

Buck teeth and black-eyed peas
Arias called Negro hymns
Bongo drum symphonies
I am from the burning house
The plantation they are still farming
Of nightshade abortions
And meagre portions
And the dream nobody knows they are harming.

I am from daughters born to mothers
Who were barely even daughters
I am from spirits that broke down
Long before birthing waters

1864

Halls is flocked on all sides by seas of cotton.
Its history is not forgotten.
It permeates every nail and needle and bale of hay.
Lauderdale County
had been the site of a great battle
in the midst of the civil war.
Confederate soldiers
invaded Fort Pillow
and slaughtered any Black soldiers on sight.
They refused to take them prisoner.
It was a massacre.
My several-greats-grandmother,
one of the farthest back I could find,

Collie,
was the product of a formerly enslaved mother
and a slave owner.
During the civil war,
she lived on inherited land in Haywood County.
I will never know the full story,
but I often wonder if her brothers who fought
were murdered by their own unknowing siblings.
Harrod J Anderson had two bloodlines.
And two daughters who bore children in the same year.
1864.
The same year his sons went to war against each other.

PART TWO

Wash Day and No Soap

1878–1940

Ninnis, b. 1878

Ninnis married Frank the same year she gave birth to Nannie
     Pearl.

By now, this was beginning to look like my family's legacy,
     shotgun weddings.
Her family,
fresh off the heels of freedom,
still lived on a farm in Haywood County.

The rest of the world
seemed oceans removed from the South
that was still rebuilding itself from the war.
She was twenty years old when she married.
Not such a far cry from girlhood.
I think that maybe our tradition
of early
weddings lies in the minds of girls
with awakened bodies, but untaught minds.

Railway Stop, 1882

Halls came into the nineteenth century

flying like lies from the mouth of a sinner.
Born as a railway stop

a decade before the birth
of Nannie Pearl it
bloomed into a town that bustled
like life had seldom done before.
The station was alight with the new era.

Finally free from the civil war
Halls was searching for a beginning.
Most of my family
spent their time sharecropping and otherwise farming.
I know this because
I found the white man who owned Ninnis's family line.
Despite Ninnis's
ten siblings, it's said that life on the farm was the same day
    after day.
You got up in the morning with the sun,
chopped the cotton,
fed the pigs,
drew the water from the well.
The men collected wood for the fire.
The girls learned what it meant to be women.

They hid periods like secrets,
they tore up old clothes
to make pads
that they washed and dried
and reused time after time.
The only things that changed
were your body and the seasons.

Nannie Pearl, b. 1898

came into the world
at the same time as a brand new century.
She learned to read and write,
tend house,
and for the first time in our family's history,
she attended school.
She lived amidst a flurry of siblings,
and they lived on their own land.

Children had the fretful souls of the grown
long before their bodies caught up
to the darkness in their eyes.
She attended school every so often,
at the one-room schoolhouse in St. Luke's church.
The classes were full of kids of every age,
who walked miles from around the district
for even the dregs of knowledge
that the rural South had to give.
Nannie Pearl woke up in the morning
in a one-room house,
flocked on all sides by siblings.
She snuck to the wood-fired stove beside her mother
to concoct meals from whatever
the earth sent their way.

Biscuits slathered in gravy
and maybe fatback.
Enough to feed the dozens of mouths around the house,
and she tended to ten rows of cotton before setting off.
In the schoolhouse,
she found arithmetic, writing,
and history if she was lucky.
And in the end, she went home.

The hot air whipped
as she was walking never stopping
there were no roses only cotton
which she needed to get to chopping
and the night
looked much the same as the morning.
Warming homegrown food over the wood fire.

In the only photo I have ever seen of her,
she holds a baby high
and wears a gentle smile;
her collar is tall and still,
her cuffs are linked
and she is a portrait of an era.
A chef from a farmer,
a woman unrelenting in her pursual of tomorrow.
She was taken as a second wife at just twenty-two
    years old.

Unsurprisingly, her eldest son
Ortho B was born just five months later.
With all these babies made out of wedlock
I'm shocked that there were any shotguns
left in the entirety of Haywood County.

No Soap 1918

Nannie Pearl and her eleven children
lived in a place in Haywood County called the Bottom.
A little spot of land
inherited from Brinkley when he died.
His parents had been sharecroppers
who came into the land
with the death of the white man
who had been their enslaver.
It is not far-fetched to assume
that one of his parents had been the man's child.
A white woman lived on the other side in a two-story house.
She said,
"Now Nannie, all them babies can't fit in that house down
    there."
After all
it was three bedrooms wide
for twelve people to share.
The white woman said,
"When I die, I'll sell you mine."
And she kept her promise.

Nannie bought the land and the plot across the wide dirt road.
The other white people around
the not quite town found
every excuse to try and stop her.
But she persisted.

Gentry sat a bright young girl
and admired her momma's prowess for business.
She learned the lesson,
"If you don't own this land, it will own you."
She learned that land was money, was power,
was doing anything a man could do.
They farmed it with only one mule and all
but Gentry still attended school,
and to this very day,
that land is in our family.

No one can take it away.
It is a monument to a woman
who charged into the future
bearing a cross and a middle finger.

Ortho B, 1921

was drafted into World War II at twenty-one.
When he came home,
they say something was missing and broken.
He searched for what he had lost overseas at the bottom of a
    bottle.
In the filter of a cigarette.
One night sleep overtook him and cigar flame and liquor met.

Curtise, Hazel, and Minnie were left to look on
as the only home they had known
went up in flames.
As the fire tore through their family
Nannie Pearl's only thought
was getting Ortho B out alive.
The blaze chomped through the life
she had built like country hounds,

on the muddy ground
outside their family's land.
All she cared for was Ortho Ortho Ortho.
And that is motherhood.

Letting some parts of yourself burn, to save others.

Sample Cakes, 1930

Nannie Pearl made the most bodacious sample cakes in
   Haywood County, Tennessee.
A sample cake is an example
of a more ample cake
it's the small spatter of the first batch of batter
used to make sure the dough flows just right.
Don't mistake a sample cake
for the full-length feature
they feel different.
Better.
They're imperfect
like people,
and the odd pockets of flavor make them sweeter.
Nannie Pearl would pass out the slices to the children,
to test if the level of fluff was just enough,
if it was moist.
If it was perfect for the white people who hired her.
The white folks
would pay Brinkley to go all the way to Memphis
to cook for the same people
by whom his family was enslaved.
The kids would seldom eat the samples

Brinkley made before he went away.
They said they didn't have no flavor.

Brinkley; Abridged. 1940

Brinkley,
before he died,
was often sent by white people to Memphis
to learn to make tasty white people pastry.
He was known for his skill with an oven or a grill.
He was a godly man.
He was a schoolteacher.

And the white people's baker.

Brinkley was the father of all of rural Haywood County.
He built the one-room wooden schoolhouse Tina Turner
    attended
on the same lot as the church that he loved so much
it killed him.
Brinkley was a soldier in many wars.
Brinkley swore to the Lord he would open the church doors
come hell or high water, but when high water came
and he went away
he left behind a daughter.

We rarely consider the girls who are left in the wreckage
of our valiant men's
reckless
decisions.

Gentry was thirteen when her father died of pneumonia.
She tried so hard to help her mother
with her ten sisters and brothers,
but there is only so much a child can do.
She tried *so hard*.

In the early mornings when the dawn swept the many
    Williams children away
down to the schoolhouse on St. Luke's
Gentry would lurk behind.
Packing up lunches and laundry,
she moved through the house like an apparition.
"WHO IS THAT?" Nannie Pearl would bellow,
throwing her voice down the hall to meet the sounds.
In return, she was often met with a meek face
peeking through double doors and a murmur.
"It's me, Momma, it's Gentry."
She was a young mother
far before she ever bore a child.

PART THREE

THE STORY OF GENTRY:
TELL THE TRUTH AND
SHAME THE DEVIL

1930–1946

Dinner 1930

In the light of the stove,
she would check the texture
of the beans
her momma had set on the fire in the early morning.
She would mash the ham hock
with a wooden spoon
so her siblings couldn't fight over
the bigger chunks.
And she set out making hot water
cornbread with her already calloused hands.
She and Corline would gossip,
Gent,
did you hear that Ethel May Wilkins
and the Cullens boy are gettin' married?
Where you hear that?
School! They was talking about it after arithmetic. You think
    she pregnant?
I wouldn't be surprised.
What a shame. She was nice.

Gentry Dancing 1932

Gentry loved to dance.
She would do the truckin

with such passion
you'd think she was entranced.
She came alive in movement.
She grew up without a father
so there was no one to stop her
from wearing the shortest skirts in the flock.
When the freedom was placed in her hands
she chased the chance to skip and jive and hop.
She *wanted to be a kid.*
She had barely gotten the chance.
She had to be her sisters' and brothers'
second mother
before she ever learned to dance.
But now, she knew how,
and all she wanted was the chance
to boogie.
Gentry grew up playing hopscotch.
She would sit on the floor
and keep score
as her brothers played stickball.
Flowing from inning to inning,
with Ortho B always winning,
either because he cheated

or because he was bigger.
I ain't feeding the chickens! Mabel would yell.
I did it last time! would be Hazel's reply.
And Mabel would check for Momma
then yell some more,
and Hazel would cry,
and inevitably,
Gentry would end up feeding the damn chickens.
Like she always did.
In the few moments of reprieve,
she would crank up the porch radio,
and listen to the stations from Memphis,
and just, *Dance.*
Take a moment to be unencumbered
by chores
or life or
even shoes.
Barefoot on the mottled porch,
she would move free.
And when the kettle whistled
or the siblings arrived home
from school the moment would end.
And she would take a rag to her feet,
turn off the radio,
and go on,
like it was a second that passed
faster than it takes
for your eyes to close and reopen.

This Frightening Change

Bloody rags crafted from a childhood nightgown
Pomegranates
Juiced either sweet or metallic.
Trash cans fill faster
Adhesive clings to your thighs like last night's liaison
The clerk at the five-and-dime asks, are you the Williams girl?

Gentry says yes, but thinks, no, no, I'm a woman.

Momma Flute 1920–2017

Momma Flute was one of those people
Who taught you how to love
One of those mommas who said you'd always be enough

She was a fighter, spirit fire: from bones to smile

The kind that makes you want to stay awhile

Momma Flute,
Also known as
Floydia B,
Always made sure the kids had enough to eat
And if she was hungry she'd smoke a cigarette
Because if *you* had enough, she's full of heart instead

Midnight Women, an Alternate Reality, the Past to the Present Day

Somebody asked me if the midnight women would lighten
With the sunrise
If Negro would just melt away
With the onslaught of day
If dawn would make
Ivory of us all

Sometimes I think it would be better if it did
If you could shake off your Black
Like a bad memory
Like an afterthought
That only in those rolling curves of gold in the sunset
Would I be
Unacceptable

That's how we have always loved
Like we were secrets
Like we exist only in the moments
That you can't illuminate
3 AM promises that you will never
Consummate

If only
Then just maybe
You would still love us when the morning comes

Gentry Pregnant, 1939

Gentry knew a bad time was coming
when her rag was still stashed
in her little corner of the bedroom after two months.
With her siblings rushing about
she thought through
the seasons that had passed.
She thought of every curse word
she had ever learned.
Another addition to the long line
of inverted nursery rhymes.
First comes the baby,
then the rushed marriage,
then come the lying
to your child
and your parents.
Finally, if you're lucky, love may show up.
Gentry had picked a real bad time
to go off and catch a child.
The Depression,
though it hadn't hit their family quite as hard,
was in fuller swing than the '20s had ever been.
The farms all around them
were keeping their food for themselves,
there was no use in selling.
And if you wanted work off it,
there was no use in looking.

She wasn't sure if she loved Walter.
But dammit, she would try. It
was the moments full of dread
that made Gentry miss the walk to school.
The stretches of dirt road with nothing
but the noise of the things that live in the trees,
the wasps that whipped around like balls of fire.
The moments that weren't so harsh,
they were just walking.
But when she found herself at an altar at only fourteen,
she was terrified
that from then on, all she could do was stand still.

Walk Gentry Home, Haywood County, TN, Circa 1940

Walter's eyes were brown,
the same brown as the hickory trees
that flanked the entry to the church where she was baptized.
And through those eyes he saw her.
It's said that she was always the first skirt tail
out the door on Sunday morning.
Gentry.

She was about fourteen at the time

but in those days
fourteen was quite nearly a woman.
By the time the clock tower went round
two or three more times
Haywood County had reinvented *Romeo and Juliet*.
Young love is a fickle and fleeting beast.
They tried to make a house cat from a coon hound,
that only ever leads to pain.
The way doors slammed
through the house that day
you'd think it was a bickering old married couple
you'd be half right.
She sat on the porch and braided the raggedy hem of her
    apron
that had been bleached into a dull grey
from layers of flour and wear.

The tears were not so much sorrow as exasperation,
and she tiptoed down a frail stair
and started on the long walk home.
Home

Real home
Not the palace of make-believe
she'd made real with wedding vows
she had no way of truly comprehending.
She walked home.
Alone.

Passed the ocean of cotton on each side of the road
outside of town she found
the little wooden house with too many mouths
and a lit lamp on the porch and she for a moment was happy.
"Momma," she said as she pushed open the mesh screen door
"Whatchu doing here, Gent," Nannie Pearl chided
as she loomed over a pot of chitlins stewed by a coal-burning
    stove
"Momma, Walter ain't shit"
"Oh"
and for an hour or so it was like it always had been
Ortho B and Gent playing jacks
and Momma bringing in snacks.
There were no babies or screaming or passion.
Just the place she came from.
"Momma, I wanna come home"

"Well, baby, then you should go. It's getting dark"
"No—"
"Ortho"
Nannie Pearl turned to the man sitting on the bench at the
    too-large table, her brother
"Walk Gentry home"

Gentry spent half a century walking home.
Treading the paths back and forth
But never knocking on her
mother's door
just running away
from a thought
to a memory.
Because Girlhood is the trip
from the home you were born into
to the home you built.
It's passing from one world into the other.
It's being a daughter
to being a mother,
and she, like so many,
was locked
or maybe lost
in the in-between,
wandering.
I'm still wondering
what being a woman is.
What making a home may mean.

Shotgun Weddings 1941

My family has a time-honored tradition of shotgun weddings.
While nobody alive at this time
can speak to Nannie Pearl's story now,
I do know this much:
Ortho B,
the older brother of Gentry,
was born six months
after the wedding of Nannie Pearl and Brinkley.

Gentry married Walter D
with his big brown eyes
the same year Levell was born.
Thrown into the world in the midst of
a second great war, they made a choice.
"Well," Gentry said, "Momma won't take him."
"It doesn't have to be your momma," he replied, "maybe
    Jewell . . ."
"You know how that woman is, Walter."
"He's light enough, she'll be kind to him."
"I don't want him to grow up all colorstruck."
"I don't want him to grow up hungry."

Colorstruck

There are a few things that are known about aint (aunt) Jewell.
One. She was a bootlegger.
As a young woman, both during Prohibition and after,
she brewed bootleg liquor and helped them drink it too.
Two. She raised Walter D after his mother died in childbirth.
Three. She was "colorstruck." What we now call colorist.
According to my aunts, when they were children,
she would give beautiful porcelain dolls to Yvonne,
Gentry's only light-skin daughter.
In the same breath, she would toss the rest of the kids two or
    three dollars
and leave it at that.
I've heard she was quite kind
if you were the right shade.
But these family rifts left behind
failed to fade after she did.

Floydia B

was daughter of Cara Vee
and Mccord's mother.

She was more grand than the Tennessee river,
covered in the sharp scent like White Diamonds perfume
gardenias and lilies
She would drape herself in
the finest silk fabric vines
every Sunday.

Monette would watch her
from the corner of the daybed
in awe of her glamour.
She was so so proud to be her granddaughter.
When my mother was younger,
Floydia would take her hands in hers.
"Ohh weee," she'd say.
"I can't believe these used to fit in my hands."
And every day
my mother grew,
in the hopes that one day,
she could fill Floydia's polished leather shoes.

Stockings, Ripley, TN, 1944

A penny for some candy
A nickel lots to spare
A dime falls down a storm drain
Until there's nothing there
And in the moments when it's falling
You think that you can hear
The rushing of the air.

Cara Vee died in autumn
The sadness rolled in with chill
Nothing worth a mother
Can be left in a will
And we all crave to honor
Our maternal legacy

Somehow it felt like stockings
Would preserve her memory

But the dime fell down
The storm drain
And like confessed sin

—

Floydia's legs were bare
And goosebumped

no stockings to cover motherless skin

The Air Base

In the '40s, Halls was home to a major air base.
The planes would zip overhead like lightning bugs.
The trails filled the sky
With fluffy catfish that swam among the clouds
And weightless white elephants that walked around up high
And if you stared long enough
You could swear
just about
That somewhere up there
Ortho B was leaving messages
to tell you when he was coming home

PART FOUR

LITTLE GIRL, DON'T YOU DARE BE AFRAID TO SUCK THE MARROW FROM CHICKEN BONES

1950–1969

Kill a Love Song

My church is America in the format of a symphony.
Each measure and stanza wills the world into poetry
a melting pot not fraught by the barriers we build
to keep bridges from rising.
The only thing we have in common is God.
Poetry is a church that diffuses its uses
through understanding abuses
but it loses its power when our only avenue
is finding cadence in hateful things.
If there's no love in the words she sings
then she becomes an ethnic religion.
A hidden world of rhythm passed from
victim to victim to paper to tomb.
There's no room for globalizing
if we only ever gaze inward
away from the world we're inheriting.
My dad says no poetry is easy
but positive poetry is hard.
It's a dark world we're looking out to
but not all of its skin is scared,
to write positive poetry
is to believe one thing is understood.
We're blessed with capacity to love, do good,
and evil is popular
but compassion withstood.

Positive poetry is faith in humanity.
My God is poetry in more forms than Christianity

Baptist or Methodist the divisions are methodless.
Call him Yahweh or Vishnu Allah Buddha too
regardless of their name or many different faces
if you have poetry and love it all goes to the same place
The universe hears when you love despite the labor
Just as Jesus spun stanzas in the future's favor
That in spite of perceived different rhythms
you should listen to your neighbor
to care about his name
that prisoners have personhood
and traitors all the same.
Happy poems are hard but how we think
is the real issue. A poem may not save the world
but the one it does will miss you
if you never try.
I know it by
the way my momma answers Bruno Mars songs like phone
     calls
It's long-distance, in fact, it's beyond the grave
She's being rung by someone from the wrong side of town
the dead-gone side of town
can't help but smile when I've found that
Mr. Mars is somehow a five-foot-five medium.
Rhymed words gave my grandma an old-school ghostly
     rotary
without them, I may never know her ghost is watching me

on phantom Facebook right now spamming "yall see my
     grandbaby"
Yvonne and Gentry and millions of mothers that came before
     she.
That poetry is stronger than the grave.
A song can give a lifeline to the long-gone

And even as the lyrics to the symphony fade
I see the devil knows nothing about a love song.
The devil is popular in this day and age
In every white house and every news front page.
And he can cage a mind like ICE can cage a child
But if hell is home you don't know not to smile

Sad music consumes us, drains joy from the arts
Lucifer entombs us in top-twenty charts
But Beyoncé and Lizzo show life full of color
magic of the past we have yet to discover.
I have a million generations of mothers in my melody
A poet's heartbeat passed down from the very first century
A passport to our past in every iambic eulogy
Their memory is poetry
Sisters and brothers in arms and in family.
Happy poetry is hard but this blood has come too far
from the Congo to Clarksville to my body to some distant star
For me to not be grateful for the art that got us where we are
To every writer that made beauty with the devil's gilded
     fiddle to
Every lover that put joy into their music just a little

My church is the kind of beat that my grandmothers dreamed
A sermon made of poetry transporting to forgotten memories
And the lyrics to the songs speak of forgiving even enemies
And the dying town has children who don't know but to smile
And the poem we're inheriting seems perfect to a child
so our future will be poetry, with a major key that plays on
Because the devil fights the vision but can't kill a love song.

Advice Poem

I asked every living woman on my mother's side what advice they would give me in regard to this whole growing up thing. This is what they said.

To every
Body
In America
That is young and melanated I
Lay before you
Some advice.

1. Don't let anyone tell you what you can and can't be
2. More often than not, foundations set you free
3. Love yourself, love recklessly
4. Fuck the naysayers, do what makes you happy
5. Don't be afraid to use your voice
6. When God hands you a gift, take it
7. Do not be conquered by self-doubt
8. Too many people don't want you to make it
9. Find confidence inside yourself
10. Don't you dare let fear shake it
11. Stay true to who you are
12. Get yourself an education
13. Don't depend on anybody else to lift you above your station
14. In this world, you must observe, because some set out to harm you

15. Be safe, and be a child, change comes so fast it will alarm you
16. You have all you need to make it, God has given you your tools
17. Don't change to be like the crowd
18. Don't ever become cruel
19. You are everything you're meant to be
20. I promise. You're enough
21. Don't let creepy old men steal your joy
22. Being a young Black girl is tough
23. But through all the trials that you'll find, all the aching and the sorrow
24. Know that just because you're down today
25. Doesn't mean you'll be down tomorrow

Reckless Girls

These reckless girls
have reckless taste in men.
When my mother was a child
Yvonne took her to live in Texas
with her new husband.
Every so often
he would fling fists at her body
marking her flesh
with blue-black constellations.
He was the meanest motherfucker
you'd ever meet.
He threw the lid of the trash can
like a discus on a collision course
with my grandmother.
Yvonne kept scars like secrets
under a layer of amber perfume and cannabis.

My sister spent all of college
in a battle of wills with a man
she didn't love.
They would battle like gods
on the mount of Olympus
in her dorm room
above the subway.
Bruises on high yellow skin

rhymed
like the Lord's Prayer.
Children are bound to gain
the same chains and shames
of all the stories their parents failed to tell.

Halls Consolidated

They used to make them do physical education.
Play baseball,
old chipped bats
stabbing splinters
into fingers like spinning wheels.
In those days,
they didn't have sports bras,
only the weight
of their chest and gravity.
Told to hold it all up on their own.

Nurses would come to school
with cases of vaccinations
mystery vials of viscous liquid
that left arms aching
like they'd been playing ball all day
with just a jab.
Everything was old and secondhand.
Often they pondered if the vials were as well.

Fighting to keep up
with the white kids in spite of the cracks
in their textbooks and sidewalks.
Learning algebra.
Geometry.
Home economics.

Business.
And get this—
All the teachers were Black.

My family integrated all of Halls' white schools.
And from the very first moment
nobody wanted them there.
In the classrooms and cafeterias
people either looked through them or down on them.
Hocking loogies like bottle rockets,
sprayed with hard-shaken Coke cans.

There was only one white girl
who would brave the walk of shame
to sit at the Brown tables.
Last name Dalentine.
Who cared more for kindness than outspoken color lines.
They would watch the chaos on the news every day,
integration came, Halls consolidated went away
and as sudden as a needle jab

they had to live the other way.
They never had a Black teacher again.

The Movies 1950

When Gentry moved to the "city"
though Halls was more of a town,
when the days were short and yawning
Nannie Pearl would come on round.
She would lend a hand in canning
fruit and help to sew the quilts.
She would proudly freeze veggies and cheese
for the seasons where nourishment wilts.
She was strong, strong, strong.
They had to be.
When daughters become mothers
they don't cease to be daughters themselves.
I've learned the things we dislike
the most in ourselves
are the things we see the clearest in our children.
Nannie Pearl used to ask why the girls were so bad.
"Little girls should *not* be so bad," she would lecture.

We are doomed to repeat the mistakes
we don't own up to,
and what they keep on forgetting
is their own shotgun weddings.

One day when Nannie Pearl came to town
Aunt Janette made the mistake of saying
she was going to the movies with a boy.

She had begged for weeks for Gentry to let her go,
only for Nannie Pearl to show
and usher to her and her mother, a clear and concise
NO.
You ain't going to the movies with no boys
But, Grandmother—
If you wanna go to someplace you'll have to pick another.
We already bought the tickets!
Then you'll take your sisters and your brother.

They walked to the theatre,
in through the special door,
they scaled the steep stairs to the colored floor.
Throughout the whole film,
not so much as a hand was held.
Aunt Cynthia sat in Janette's lap
as any hopes of romance were felled.

Mothers are harshest
when their hope
is helping you avoid
making the mistakes
that had once been their own.

So a Man Thinketh So Is He

When Cynthia was a child,
her teachers were shocked a Negro could be so clean.
But Gentry kept a spotless house,
a spotless child.
She worked the skin off the tips of her fingers
raising two families.
A white one in the daylight,
her own at night.
Cleaning two homes
from baseboard to baseboard
before the sun rose.

She took night school by candlelight.
She was on a mission to finish the eighth grade.
When the times got tough,
she just worked more,
and her children say they never
even realized they were poor
until long after the time for minding
had come and gone.

Janette spent her first paycheck
as a newly minted lab tech
on a bike for Cynthia's ninth or tenth birthday.
It had polished training wheels and a basket,
a majestic gift for a youngest sister.

"Don't go riding that bike by the church door you hear."
"Yes ma'am I do promise I ain't gon' go near."
And like that her solemn vow
went out the other ear
and the first thing Cynthia did
was ride the bike
right where Gentry told her not to.

Knowing something isn't right
often isn't enough to stop you,
but a big old broken tooth will.
Cynthia spent the next fifteen years

With ½0th of a grill.

Lord Give Gentry Some New Monkeys Cause These Can't Dance

I hear the clatter of my daughters out the window at night
If they end up like their other mothers there's no chance

I remember that old sizzle of teenage romance
I'm wishing for the wisdom in the heavens' light
Lord give me some new monkeys cause these can't dance

For the lust of young years leaves you without a glance
If they end up like their other mothers there's no chance
Lord give me some new monkeys cause these can't dance

Stillborn, Haywood County, 1957

"For sale baby shoes never worn"
It's the simple things we mourn
that kill us the most inside
the stigmatized suffering we're all forced to hide
the baby-sized caskets the four-foot graves
the never-ending sorrow drowning our minds in crashing
    waves
the shallow gradient of gloom inside every barren womb
and they all told you it was never meant to be
but you felt less like a woman because no fruit bore from your
    tree

The Lacy Girls

The four Lacy girls
were a hive of queen bees
stout but strong of spirit
personalities grand like sequoia trees

wide smiles
Hair like oak wood
but Yvonne had honey skin
and hair that couldn't hold a curl
hers was tawny long and thin

they canceled prom Janette's senior year
There was too much danger of love doo-wopping over color
    lines
So they canceled it
completely so no one could be together

Make a Fool out of You 1960

The television
sat in the corner of the dining room.
A true innovation,
a twelve-inch screen,
black and white,
writhe with static.
It was the star
of the Lacy house in the year 1960.
It was like magic.
Instead of old hopscotch and kickball
they had discovered live television in lack of color.
Walter D warned
them repeatedly
to not ever fight around the TV,
but in a house of six siblings,
this rule was immediately broken.
Over a piece of chicken.
Jacqui and Yvonne skirted around the edge of the table
laying out forks and plates for Gentry
to come behind and pile them high
with cornbread and veggies.
In the moments after Gentry
laid the pan with the fried chicken
in the center of the table disaster struck.
"I want the thigh."
"But I was supposed to get it."

"I'm older."
"It's my turn!"
Yvonne leapt from her chair
to gain leverage on the poultry
when the back of her chair
collided with the screen of the TV.
The world held their breath as the stand rocked.
Relief washed over the family like warm gravy when it became
    still.
"Okay," Walter said,
and removed the chicken from her shaking hands.
"This right here is mine now.
And you," he said, wielding a finger at Yvonne.
"Good night, I hope dat chicken was worth it!"
Jacqui tried to hide a snicker
and quicker than she could blink she met the same fate.
It was the whole next day
before any chicken got ate.

Cotton Picking 1960

Gentry was no stranger to the cotton field.
She chopped
to the tune of Sammy Davis
as she worked her way through the rows.
Baby Cynthia rested high
upon a pile of
cotton in her cotton bag,
giggling and sputtering
into the air like it was a day's adventure.

But in the depths of the ocean
of soft white lurked a cottonmouth.

It slithered towards the baby set to bite her
but the snake was no match for a mother.
Gentry grabbed it by its throat
and threw it clean across the field.
And left the cotton for tomorrow
until the pain of *almost* was healed.

The Birth of a Young Son, Halls, TN, Circa 1960

God help me I've got fragile boys
they've all got paper skin
wrong words can break their plastic hearts
and glass bones. Within
my beautiful boys,
they're porcelain.
They float in pools of green and blue
only I can see through
the bubbles of depression that surround.
My boys have got no confidence
Not a drop to be found.
I can't help it I draw fragile boys
with cracks all through their past
I pray that when they let me go
I won't be the last.
These fragile boys they tear me down
because I'm trying to build them up.
My soul's running on empty
not a drop left in my cup.
My boys have got jealousy
my boys have got rage
my boys have got pain
far beyond their age.
They seem to have forgotten
completely how to trust,
and they don't make a sound

when you turn them all to dust.
God bless my little fragile boys
for I don't know what to do.
They pull at my heart from every angle,
my heart is still clay
they don't know
it can mangle—
I use it to fill the cracks that
form on their souls.
I give up pieces of me
to make them whole.
God damn my little fragile boys
I love them all the same.
I pray for freedom.
For all the little joys
but I give up all I have
to save my broken fragile boys.

The Colored Prom, 1960

At the colored prom the year prior, Janette wanted to be like
   all her friends out on the town. To traipse the
   neighborhood in her long yellow gown.
She lied and said she could go to eat at a Ripley joint down the
   street. Even though she knew she couldn't.
"naw you know Ms. Gentry don't like you being in cars with
   no boys," said Anderson, her most recent toy.
"no no she said i could go." So off they went, Janette in tow. To
   Ripley for a hot sock hop, a colored-friendly restaurant
   truck stop.
But when she got home the house was lit up inside and out.
   Gentry had called every parent that she knew. She came out
   of the house in her fighting clothes with her overalls and
   her head rag on lopsided.
"open the door for me," Janette said.
"naw get out yourself, she got on her fighting clothes."
The boys put her out the car and drove
into the darkness.

Black Sheep

Grandma Yvonne
was a light-skinned black sheep.
She never quite fit in with the rest. They would taunt and tease
"There's no way your daddy could really be Walter D"
"There's no way these could be your sisters and brothers"
"You're high yeller"
"You're—"
"You're—"
"You're—"
And when she fell heavy with child
the only taunt was
"Whore."
Mccord wouldn't marry her.
He would not propose,
he left her to hear the taunts and jeers
that recklessly arose
but he was just sixteen
a boy
in a moment that slams doors closed.
He was college bound,
a full ride to play ball,
but a baby in the making
makes sky high dreams fall.
A moment's notice
to become a husband
doesn't turn a boy into a man.

But a ring on a teenage finger
could have gotten a shunned girl an open hand.

Yvonne wasn't very good at staying with hobbies.
She joined the cheer squad
but never learned a single dance.
She joined the marching band
and lip-synched
on the clarinet like she was playing concertos,
yet never
blew a single breath through the reed.
She lived in a world inside her head
away from all the chaos at the campus,
and the perfectly in-line
life she didn't fit into at home.
She was never good at running
anywhere but in her own mind.
Sometimes it's easier to escape
into brains than cityscapes.
More often than not, no place
can free you from the cages
you're placed in
because the world is the world is the world.
And if you have enough color,
just living shatters fantasies.

Church

Gentry made sure her daughters went to church,
and Bible study too.
Even on the hot summer days
when all you wanted to do was lay
in the grassy patch beside the blacktop

and let the condensation cool your skin
in tandem with the pooling sweat.
Where all the kids from the block
would lay in their own spot,
those with fresh-pressed hair
propped up on stacks of books
looking to the clouds
for a whisper of shade.
Everyone would be waiting in anticipation for the ice cream
that Mrs. Gentry made,
a constellation of children laid on the ground,
chalk lines drawn between Chucks
and penny loafers that had long been
abandoned by the feet they were made to adorn.

The Chaperone

Mccord and Bill
were best friends
and at the rate they were going
soon to be brother-in-laws.
Every weekend they would spend time
at the coolest teen place
out in Ripley
on a double-and-a-half date.
Bill and Jacqui, Mccord and Yvonne, and . . . Cynthia.
Cynthia was the sanctioned chaperone
of all her more grown sisters.
By declaration of Gentry
when Yvonne and Jacqui
would go on dates they would have to take her along.
They would play pool and dance and pay nine-year-old
    Cynthia
to mind her business.
She would sit in the corner and watch the teenage
    mayhem.
Often the boyfriend of a girl
named Janice
who couldn't come to the club
would pay her to stay quiet
about his dancing with other young lovers.

And the next day Janice would pay her to speak up.
She would sit back and watch the chaos,
clutching a popsicle,
a true entrepreneur.

Yvonne Pregnant, 1969

Momma Gent knew Yvonne was pregnant before Yvonne.
Promptly
every Monday she did
laundry
and sorted the pairs of shirts and underwear
based on the initials stitched within them.
She counted the period panties
on the off chance. Just in case.
So none of her daughters made her mistakes.
In the fall of 1969
Gentry's worst nightmare came alive

with a missing pair of drawers,
belonging to one Yvonne Lacy.
You see, Yvonne Lacy
had been crawling out the window lately
to go visit her boyfriend
in the silent hours of the night.
She was a freshman and he was a senior.
She had a more mature demeanor.
And through the darkness,
after heart-to-hearts, Jacqui
would let Yvonne back in,
after all it was none of her business
what had happened
and she was just helpin',

and that's what good sisters do.
This is of course exactly
what my sister Alayna would tell you.
Janette and Jacqui
would jest and laugh
about how Yvonne would become
rotund and ugly and fat,
and the whole town went on about how
she was *Bad bad bad.*
She was the "never enough"
they always believed her to be.
When she began to show

the kids about town stopped meeting her eyes in the halls.
One dewy Sunday morning
she was forced to stand before
the entire congregation of her church
and profess her "sins,"
she bore herself to be chastised
in spite of the words Jesus proselytized.
"Let he who is without sin cast the first stone,"
they who swore to live lives of love
piled rocks to tear down a girl
who only ever wanted to feel less alone.

The Only Pool in Ripley

Lordy be! Yvonne screamed dancing around the immaculate
    house
I know he whispered.
He took her hand
Follow me
they glided through the high arches and pillars to the back
    patio
Where polished stone covered the expanse of land up to the
    edge of the pool.
Ta-da Mccord said
Motioning to the crystalline blue of the pool.
It's beautiful
Then what are you waiting for he said discarding his shirt to
    the ground
for a moment she faltered but she slipped off her shoes and
    dipped her toes into the water
I can't she paused
Swim? he said
Yeah there was never anywhere for me to learn, or a reason to
    know I guess, it's dumb
Hey he said cradling her face in his hands never talk about
    yourself like that, you're perfect he leaned down and placed
    a slight kiss on her lips.
Plus, that's what hot tubs are for

She averted her eyes and shied as he shed the rest of his
    clothes and
slipped into the bubbling waters
You coming in?
I promise I won't let you drown

Keep Living

"I promise
"I will never ever be like you
"Keep living don't ever say
"what you're not going to do"

PART FIVE

Show Me the Company You Keep I'll Tell You Who You Are

1971–1999

Good Girls

There are certain people in our family
who worked hard to be good girls.
Good girls are the anxious kind.
The kind that work so hard to be perfect
in the hopes that they will ever be enough.
My grandmother was a fair-weather parent.
She was fleeting like seasons,
never an empty tank in her car.
In the early mornings
she would drive to her mother's house
and send Monette and Little John off to ring the doorbell.
When the porch lights flipped on
she would speed off down the street
to whatever adventure it was
she was chasing that day.
Aunt Jewell would do the same.
Then Casey,
now Lacy,
it's a legacy of pain.
My family has spent centuries in search of girlhood.
Even when it came only in the form of running from being a
    woman.

The Day It Happened

If gunshots were blessings would our bodies be holy
If the Bible had Black idols would these people pray
If chains were some kind of divine matrimony
Would you shun us from your heaven anyway?

Bunny Rabbit, 1976

When my mother was little
she and her cousins would play the guessing game.
Maybe we'll get her this time, she would whisper to Aundrea
It never worked before
she can always tell,
she may be old as dirt,
but she knows her children well.
Well, I would like to try
She went up to Nannie Pearl and asked
Whose daughter am I?
she would say
they were Gentry's kids
and that they had to be from one of her daughters
and that my momma
was Bunny Rabbit's baby.
My mother had never known
Yvonne had a nickname
until they played the guessing game.
She used to call Yvonne Bunny Rabbit
because she had two big old ponytails
on either side of her head.
They flopped about as she sang
and spoke in floppy rabbit ears' stead.
When Yvonne was young
she would suck her thumb

like she was making up for lost time imbibed from
    a bottle.
Bunny Rabbit.
Always going fast.
Hopping away to another sight of life.

The Day Mccord Died, Just 25, Ripley, TN, Circa 1976

Yvonne finds iron sky
She breathes withered vines
She chokes on unworn lace veil lines
Out of sight on her mind

Misguide her tightened spines
Tense face tendrils blind
Tears dare to tug
Her eyes
Safe to never say denied
She watched the battered door
Never loved the sand before
It digs easy

Bury herself some more
You hid her skin
To suffocate your sin
You never said
"Be my bride"
"Be my bride"
Disappeared
Dissatisfied.

St. Louis, 1977

The day Yvonne left for St. Louis,
Monette already knew she wasn't going.
But the sadness still filled
every moment
because she knew Yvonne
would be taking the baby.
Johnny, her brother, her baby.
It was one of those times
that end
before you've really comprehended
what is happening,
and you're left feeling relentlessly alone.

1977, Halls, TN

Did you see her on the news—
You see him on the news—
Did you hear about the news—

The news—
News—
He had a daughter at seventeen
A basketball star turned line-of-duty casualty
She was left the bearer of a legacy
Whether it's a teenage pregnancy

Or talent hidden in memory for centuries

I'm not sure what it means
I wonder if people are lost
When they're dead
If the news
Keeps on living
In a loved one's
Stead

The Blood the Blood the Bride

A ring on a finger's a noose
The poison you choose
The way that you kept the demon off the loose
The love was the muse now you've got the blues
The marriage a cage not a passion a truce
You don't think I see how you take the abuse
I saw how each kiss would turn into a bruise
Your life is all you got left now to lose

The ring is the box
where you keep your contagious self-hatred
you learn from the pain
you learn from the lies
and you learn how to play it
you yearn for the days
back when you were set for a garbage bin grave you master the
    stage
and you come to hide the homegrown slave how you've been
    bound
you miss your black plastic funeral gown.
No kind words to say when they lowered you into the ground
But you've never been the best at goodbyes.
That's why you're stuck with the boy with the blue eyes.
We're all praying that you make it out alive.
True love is not something you should barely survive.

Green Piano 1980

At my great-grandmother's house,
there was a green piano.
You see, in the country
there wasn't much to do,
so in the heat of the summer
all the cousins would gather around the piano.
My mother would play the keys
and from there they would sing for hours.
Only stopping to change players.
Flooding the streets with the most joyful kind of noise.
Places are like shoes,
you grow in them and you grow into them,
and eventually, you grow out of them.
But moments like those
summers frozen in time
are old sweaters.
They were always far too big for the moment.

Monette

Monette marched in the high school band in eighth grade.
She was a 4'11" pocket of stardust.
She played the piano and the clarinet,
conducted the band,
sang like Aretha Franklin on stage,
and most of all she was lonely.
When she was younger
the traveling salesman came to town,
and she acquired an entire set of encyclopedias
and a little white book.
By the time she began
learning to read, Mccord had died and Yvonne
had gone on a long drive
to anywhere but where
Monette needed her to be.
The little white book
was a step-by-step guide
on teaching yourself to read,
and she did indeed,
alone in the room
waiting for the world to want her.
She and the book were very best friends.
They sat together in special education
where she was placed
when the teachers wouldn't dare to face
the fact that she wasn't stupid,

she was just learning all on her own.
As a matter of fact
nobody knew she was in special education
until the day she tested out.
And then,
she found a new best friend,
the green piano.
On good days she would play,
and on bad days she would play,
and she would play and play
until the music made the hurting fade.

Loneliness is the loudest thing there is.
It's the kind of feeling that eats through good moments.
It teeters at the edge of your field
of view until you fall headfirst into it.
Lonely is the melancholy
that a sweet leaves in the back
of your throat.
It covers good memories like the worst haze,
and even when the lonely does,
the fog never fades.

Independence, 1980

The word Momma Gent lived by
was independence.

She worked relentlessly.
Right after she left for Halls she began
keeping house for a white family.
She did extra laundry
for the white folks
if the kids needed money for something,
and she absolutely refused to sit still.

Her house stayed spotless,
polished from edge to edge,
just like her mother's.
She took care of the kids,
and for the sake of her baby,
she put up with Walter D's dear
colorist, reckless Aunt Jewell.
In the summers
Monette and her cousins would help her package
massive hauls of Stanley Home creams and butters
degreasers and steel scrubbers
in brown paper bags for her customers.
They would take the bags out to the sidewalk
of 415 Fenton Street
and deliver the goods straight to the car.

They sang as they bagged
and ran and made games out of the work.
The tables would be labeled and she would tell them
Now girls, if you want anything in life, you gotta go after it.
She would show off her trophies for being the top seller and
remind them to always remember.
Nothing can stop you but *you*, child.
So a man thinketh, so is he.

Patches of Green, Ripley, TN, 1984

Have you ever seen the orange sky,
just before the storm?
It's a daunting beautiful high,
but its grandeur is forlorn.
As when the water falls,
it's bleached to grey,
the same color we mourn.
Have you ever seen the way
blood bounces on the snow?
It melts into the pristine ground
but freezes in its flow.
Have you ever seen the child
who inherits a burning empire?
Left to handle the plights of his forefathers
they collapse as soon as he does tire.
Have you ever witnessed injustice
of which you'll never know?
Phantom chains on ancestral wrist
they blessed you to never tow.
Have you ever seen a siren's face?
It holds a mouth that births sacred sound
but her music is justly debased
when you learn it was she
who burned the child's empire down.
On this little blue dot,

with its patches of green,
there's so much,
so much,
We have never seen.

As Man and Wife, 1984

Monette learned Yvonne and James Tyus were married
when she was fourteen.
In a classroom, just in passing,
her classmates walked by laughing.
"I heard your momma got married"

buried in the sea of chatter.
Buffy knew of Yvonne's beau
before her own daughter.
How do you even handle
the news of a new father?
Eloping.

It's the notion that your life can change in only a moment.
That one second you're single,
the next you're buried in an era of we,
instead of I.
She didn't even ask Monette's permission.
Stepparents are the rare kind of person
who you're stuck with before you grow to love them.
They're a stranger in your home
who takes time to move into your heart.
It's an arranged marriage.
One a child doesn't get to consent to.
But every so often
you uncover an extra father or mother

who will love you
like they've spent all of your life
with you
and my grandpa James Tyus
is the only one I've ever known.
And even if there's no blood between us,
he will always be Home.

Drive, 1985

When you let the world define you,
you become what the world defines you as.
When Yvonne took Aundrea
on the long drive back to Bunkie, Louisiana,
she used the only thing the world says she has.
When they were speeding
stopped by a cop off the edge of highway nineteen
She said
Watch
Getting a ticket ain't exactly my thing.
She shimmied down her neckline,
flipped her wild hair,
and flirted with the policeman
until the 50mph sign wasn't even there.
And as they kept on down the roads
She taught them bodies can be shields
Or weapons
Or cages
That keep the you in you
From driving back.

District 10, Haywood County, Always

We grew up alongside the weeds
In district 10
Haywood County
In the summers, the truck
Would pick us up and we'd
Pick cotton for pocket money

Aunt Mabel lives on a farm in
Haywood County
Our family owns that land
And we're afraid to say why
Afraid of the people
Out beneath the cotton fields
Who had to die for us
For her to build a marble house
In district 10 Haywood County
Momma was supposed to be a
Child bride in district 10
Haywood County
Our legacy is crusted blood
Atop ancient thighs in
District 10 Haywood County
My momma said that when
She dies,

when she dies
keep her far away.

Life of It

Yvonne was the life of the party.
And when she was ready to leave
she would sneak out the back door,
and the fire would fade
before anyone had time to realize
what had changed.
She was never much for the rhythm,
never much for the melody,
but boy oh boy,
would she harmonize

how she ripped a moment into life with the music
of her presence.
She was the scat in the jazz song.
No words,
only sounds of whimsy
at the whim of her lips
in every second she was present.
She kept no beat.
Where Gentry danced in place she would run.
She was the kind of girl
who stopped records with her words,
and ended extravaganzas when she was done.

The Choir

Aretha Franklin Queen of Soul
Breathed life back into the
Old-school song
What a friend we have in Jesus
The choir desired to bring
Zion Baptist into the new decade
They practiced day and night
Every Saturday until the streetlamps
Lit up
And when Sunday came they
Sang
The parishioners' first response
Was to toss the flock
Far from the house of the Lord
Out the door
Miss Aretha was sang inside
The church no more
Sometimes
We are not ready for the changes
That are ready to come.

The Most Judgmental Women Are Those Who Hate Themselves

Women were always trying to fight Monette.
And one thing that teaches you, is never forget
just how strong a tongue is.
Rumors burn up like newspaper insulation
in old schoolhouses.
A light in the dark sparks a whole house in flames.
Gentry taught Monette that gossip does the same.

In ninth grade,
all Monette wanted was to be like Christie.
She was the town beauty,
a dimple on her cheek,
knew her way around a song,
the whole of Halls
knew Christie Ashe had it going on.
She moved to Halls when her momma died
and would go to Monette's house
and hang around daily.
Yvonne and Christie's aunt were dear friends.
They would sit around in the room,
and Christie talked about boys
with Cyndi Lauper playing softly
from the boom box, background noise.
It was a simple moment.
But one day in the hall a girl named

Piper approached with a dire fire in her eyes:
"I heard you were talking about my boyfriend."
"What? No no I wasn't. Christie was there! Ask her"
Monette put her hands up
and tried to slip away; she was telling the truth.
But that never once stopped
the mobs of thought that crowd high school halls.
You could hear Piper's feet fall
as she crossed the hall to meet Christie.
Monette froze hoping for the crisis to be averted
"I have no clue what she's talking about, she's lying"
Christie blurted. And in that moment something inside
    Monette shattered.
She learned a bitter lesson that day.
Everyone remembers the first time someone looked them
in the eyes and lied on them.
Betrayed them.
It was hard to comprehend just why an older girl,
her idol,
would decide to dislike her,
would lie to spite her
when all Monette ever wanted was to be just like her

The White Dress

Monette had a white dress.
She kept it spotless and pressed,
it was the first thing that ever made her feel beautiful.
On a tepid August day Christie blew through
Halls High School's doors with her hips asway
in the very same white dress.
From the Dillard's in Jackson.
The epitome of '80s high fashion.
A grand example of self-doubts most consistent
passion never letting you have a moment
of self-compassion,
because when keeping up is all
you have there's no time for growth to happen.
It's fascinating,
how the people who hurt you in high school
can haunt you long after you've gathered your cap and gown.
If we walked past Christie on the street these days
I would never know it happened,
because Monette would never let
herself look up from the ground.

One-Sided Fights Ain't Nothin' but Abuse

A Direct Quote

"Oh, Christie! How you doing?"

"I'm fine, how 'bout you?"

"I got engaged!"

"Oh, child, I don't wanna talk about that, Sabrina already fucked your man."

Young Brides

My mom was engaged at the ripe old age of sixteen.
She inherited a different set of generational curses.
She wanted to be free of Halls.
To see the world
To skip town
But a ring gave her an anchor
Dragging a young body down.
But when he bought her a house, just across town
She knew she had to start running
Or she risked becoming
Every mother
Who never took her time
To dance.

The Daughter Will Learn, Halls, TN, Summer 1969–1981

After "Strange Fruit" by Billie Holiday and Lewis Allan

Sins might happen for a reason
One of my mothers never made it past an eighth-grade
    education
Understand that she made a choice at fourteen to start a
    generation
The sins of the father are the sins
His son will learn
Everybody believes they are the exception
Remember children will
Never do as you say

The day my grandmother learned she was pregnant she was
    seventeen
Running away from a generational curse
Education isn't worth much if it's propaganda
Everyone *knew* she was bad, cause she was high yella
Sins of a mother are sins her daughter will learn

Before my grandfather died he had a child
Everyone told him it was over
And he loved her
Regardless of how they tried to change his mind

—

Seventeen was a lifetime to my great-grandmother
Time came down like Southern rain from
Raging April skies
And when Grandpa was shot down that following July
Never again did they think you could be too young to die
Gifts don't always come in the forms you think they do
Every so often so-called sins become blessings

Fifteen, sixteen, seventeen was a lifetime
Right before disaster God brings sunshine
Underneath the skin of sinners lies divine
Insight, we are not privy to His plans until it's our
Time

Monette, Driving

The thing Monette wanted more than anything
wasn't the car,
it was the *stereo*.
She would cruise the streets of Halls
bumping all the greatest hits
of 1986
cool as an Orange Julius.
One day she was on her way
to drive Tammy to her grandmother's house
when her JAM came on.
The synthetic rhythm of Jermaine Stewart took over the tiny
   Toyota.
The lyrics "we don't have to take our clothes off to have a good
   time" blasted through the windows and into the streets of
   Halls.
Mo pressed a Mary Jane against the brake and told Tammy to
   "hop in!"
Tammy . . . rolled her eyes,
scuffed a toe against the ground, and begrudgingly complied.
And for the whole—and I do mean *the whole*—two-minute car
   ride to Tammy's Grammy's house the noise continued on.
The latest news of AIDS was quickly switched over to Cyndi
   Lauper, and with Tammy safely inside, Monette continued
   to kick it in her ride.

Y'all Need to Stop Underestimating the Evil in Somebody Just Because They Say They're a Woman of God

Ellie-May
was for all intents and purposes Monette's mentor.
She was the cheer coach and Monette her protégée.
Monette ran the whole team from drills to cheers every day.
Monette would watch her children on the weekends.
Ellie-May Fairview loved Monette.
But she would never let her forget one thing.
She was still a nigger.
Monette stood in Ellie-May's office and offered a question
"Where do you think I should go for college?"
"I say go where you'll be acknowledged,
go to UT Martin, you'll be a big fish in a little pond."
"But Miss Ellie-May,
I'm already a big fish in a little pond.
I want to see what it feels like to swim with other big fish."
"Don't get dreams too big for your head, there is always a safer
    wish."
Monette just once wanted to see what it felt like to run.
So in spite of what they said to her,
she did what no one in our family had ever done.
"I'm going to UT Knoxville."

*"We will give her a scholarship to march in our band
but she will never be a drum major and she will never try out."*

—

UTK and Ellie-May thought the same way,
she may
have been the best drum major in the entire state,
but some things exceed all.
Some never change.
They wanted her to remember.
You can work twice as hard
You can be three times better
But you will still
Be a nigger.
And they never had a Black drum major
until 2017

Miss Halls

The year Monette became Miss Halls
she had sworn
she would never compete again.
She had placed third maid so many times
that it was futile
to even try.

But her good friend Kelly wouldn't let her give up
Mo, you just gotta try,
she said.
Try one last time.
You see, this was the biggest Miss Halls they had ever had.
The former Miss Tennessee
the mother of Miss America
and the superintendent of the entire school district
would be judges.
This was a far cry from the usual panel of powder-faced,
pearl-necked mothers.

So Monette went back one last time
to try for the crown of her tiny town.
She crooned an old-school gospel
tune in a blue sequined ball gown.

In the back room with the judges
a pearl-wearing mother

from the planning committee came to state a demand.
The Black girl can place, but she *cannot win.*
If the Black girl doesn't win,
then you won't be having a queen tonight.
When they read out Monette's name
under the stage spotlight the people of Halls
booed.
They didn't care that she won fair and square.
They couldn't accept a Black girl as their Miss Halls.
To this day there has never been another.

Perm

A perm is a tool for making "nappy hair" neat and clean.
A perm is a tool for making natural hair chemical.
A perm is a tool for changing yourself just like any other.
My mother gave every daughter she had a relaxer when we
    reached the seventh grade.
Her mother never had a curl to spare.
They said Yvonne had that "good hair."
I suppose those words really said that what spun from my
    head was bad.
In the '80s
Yvonne and Tammy's mother stood side by side and tried to
    apply a perm to Tammy's hair.
They pulled on each side of her head and applied their own
    toxic share.
Tossing compliments back and forth over the crown of their
    shared child.
A duo determined to make the young girl's fro less wild.
Less

Bad bad bad
Combing out every last ring of Blackness that Tammy had.
Not because her color was stored in her curls
But because you had to be straight of hair
To be a good girl.

The Soprano

They say you could recognize Aundrea's singing voice
clean across town.
She, Monette, and Casey used to
sing in a group all around
West Tennessee.
Her crisp soprano
could rip tears from anyone's eyes.
When she was in high school
she found herself in the role of Elizabeth
in a production of *Twelve Years a Slave* the musical.
They tell me that when she would sing the world would stop.
I ask her when the last time she sang was
And when she answers, I wonder,
This world spins so fast
why would you not hold every note to stop it?

Everybody knew when the Payton girls were coming to Halls.
They were the hot topic among the boys
every summer when Janette's old van
would pull onto Fenton Street.
The boys,
in preparation for their arrival
would part ways with their 9–5 girlfriends
for the chance at fabled summer flings.
Every year
Monette would plead please

Don't take my classmates' mans
because once you're both gone
I'm the one left to stand and fight.
And Sondra would say,
Of course I won't, and Aundrea would say,
Well. I might.

Labor Day

Labor Day was the party of the year.
The bouncy houses on the blacktop
shined like beacons
summoning family from every corner
of the country.
From sun up to midnight
for three days straight the whole town came alive.
Every chef brought a booth
or a truck and passed out barbecue
and wings and snow cones
so dense with syrup
you could use the dregs at the bottom
to flavor a ten-cent Sprite.
In older times we would gather at Gentry's house
and lie at her feet enjoying
every moment together
like time was frozen.
In later times we gathered at Yvonne's.
Now we gather at a house where we lie at the feet of a
    phantom.
No one mentions how we gather around an empty chair.

Geology

When you were little you wanted to be a geologist
To study rocks and their making, how the world has changed
Since they were crafted in the magma womb of the earth
Sometimes people throw your rocks away.
And you bid dreams like these goodbye
Dreams often tend to fade
But they never truly die.

You Ain't Gotta Die and Go to Heaven or Hell to Get What You Deserve, Part I

Kayla was a bully.
It's hard to escape girlhood without encountering one
without being one yourself.
Whenever she would push Amber to the ground
Amber found herself frozen.
Gentry gave her some words of wisdom.
The next time she puts her hands on you? Hit her back.
I know, it sounds hard but see,
there was a girl just like Kayla who used to mess with me,
and I promise, when you fight back once,
they'll never mess with you again.
Bullies are cowards.
And in the vital hours when victims become empowered,
people like Kayla cower when faced with what they inflict on
   others.

Growing

When you are growing
It feels like every time you catch up with the buildings they get
    bigger
Like in high school there are solar systems and atoms and
Sex and drugs with so many names you can't tell if
Mary Jane is a classmate or a crime
This world is loud
It's funky, holding smells that drip from adolescent bodies
Like slurs on tongues.
And you will feel like being enough means being a part of it
And when you're a part of it enough is just the start of it
And the words turn into acts that turn to shame
And once you're all grown up
The world's size feels the same.

Show Me the Company You Keep I'll Tell You Who You Are, Part II

The party was alive.
It was pounding through the speakers
shaking the ground
to the tune of Deee-Lite
like the whole block had caught the holy spirit.
On a night like this you might stumble across your boyfriend
    driving another girl's car.
You see when the party's jumpin' but you're hopelessly lonely
    you just gotta wonder where the one you can hold be if he's
    off down the block bumpin' and grindin' on a shawty,
a shawty, and you wonder, is she better than me?
And when you see them driving past
you on the long walk home you'll see
shawty in the passenger seat
drunk, out cold, and you'll pray.
That your boyfriend was only doing a good deed.
That the somber notes on his face don't tell the story that you
    read.
That you don't need to call Dianne's momma
just in case there are lines
he hadn't had the time to cross yet.
But the world is just *is*, not if, and if into the dark they do drift
you know the holy ghost in the notes of groove is in the heart,
couldn't even start to save her.

Smoke

The blacktop
stayed busy crowded
with the kids who planned to sneak off to Ripley.
To party grind the music,
cloud out cerebellums with cannabis.
Color your lungs green
like all in the world you needed
was to steal Christmas.
Shotgun. Blow smoke rings in your face.
Lie in the streets lit up
by mostly broken streetlamps
chance the hot tarmac against your skin
for a brief reprieve from gravity.
Higher than Cooter Brown.
Breathe in the forest you run to
when the cops come
and hum a Lauryn Hill song
in tune with the flashing of the fireflies.

Bobos

Miss Alice had a habit of adding beads
to braids
no matter the age of the hair wearer.
Jordania and Amber were nineteen when their heads
were filled with pink and blue jewels for the last time.
Miss Alice told them
You know, being young ain't a crime.
Don't run from being a child.
Being a woman will still be there when you get back.

Colonizers, 1990, Knox County, TN

Our bodies were colonized for many lifetimes
Our tongues, our heads, our thighs
But after the fight for civil rights we realized they'd
Colonized our minds

PART SIX

THE STORY OF ALORA

2002–Present

A Letter from the Womb, Teaneck, NJ, 2002

Build me a body on my bones craft a skeleton
Breathe me a life
Let me rattle in my rib cage
Who I was before the papier-mâché
Begging for oxygen
Breathe me life
Give me glue lungs
My nerves on glitter
PVC pipe femurs
The hollow rattle
They ache for marrow
The airplane the box car
The cage
The recycled air
Five miles high
Breathe me life
And I promise I will leave you

Summer

This is joy.
This is chasing my dog back and forth
across the living room
lying on the carpet,
nap time,
blacktop
parties in Philip's attic
this is every moment on stage.
This is hitting the right beats.
This is penne alla vodka
the blacktop,
pizza from the Exxon
the bread coming out perfectly risen.
This is touch me.
This is she's such a sweetheart
riding down highway nineteen on roads without names,
this is the first time I got doped up
This is the swing set
This is the first day without panic attacks.
Sopping up the gumbo
with rice and beans
Picking the strawberry fields clean
direct deposit in my checking account,
eighth grade,
the last time I saw my grandmother,
happy and alive alive alive.

Halls, Depleted

You used to be able to go downtown and see a city alive.
The five-and-dime, three grocery stores,
more things to do than people to do them,
but Halls followed the rhythm of the world around it.
It was founded on the railroad,
then the railroad died,
next it had a grand old factory
that fell by the wayside.
Despite how they tried
they couldn't catch up.
Halls is a living bit of history,
and despite all the falling-down houses it's found a way
to be what America dreamed.
A place where you know your neighbors' names.
Where Black and white play the same.
Where there is no place to be vain or put on airs
because there's always someone who was there
when your dirty laundry was made.
You are comfortable with who you are because
you can't hide in the shade.
Where if you stop by the blacktop
you're sure to find a friend,
and no matter if you're tied by blood
they will be your family till the end.
You have compassion for every last citizen,
you have hospitality,

no matter your past you're welcomed in.
In the olden days it was the big city.
It's my heart it's where I began.
It's a part of me that's dying but it always lives within.
The story of America fades with every citizen
because it was America.
In a place far off the path.
In a moment.
There is no more rich a place in history,
with more knowledge of the world,
that knows the past of womanhood,
what it means to be a girl
than the rusty terra-cotta colored streets
lined with monuments, abandoned pictures of history.
Every moment, a closed store from 2020 to 1864.
There is nary a better pathway
to the worlds and worlds that lived before
than Halls.

Darkskin/Lightskin 2008, Davidson County, TN

My sister is a fruitful soil
Like my mother is a fruitful soil
Like I am clay
Like her mother was
Like if you set me on fire I will harden
Like a statue, always trapped in the
In-between
If you burn her
Rich dark earth
The mother of all life all beauty
She simply bears better fruit

Sister, Sister

Sisterhood is not as lovely as one would have you believe.
There is something to be said for
the war of wills between two girls
with faces almost the same
who will spend forever
enraptured in a combat of passions,
and looks.
My sister hates my sister
almost as much as Yvonne's sisters
hated her.
Sisterly hatred is special.
It brews itself in silence. It's seasoned by jeers from your
    peers of
She's cuter because she's light-skinned.
She's smarter.
She's kinder.
She's the pretty twin.
Ugly twin.
Every pubescent moment
is saddled with a battle against
your own mind.
But in schoolhouses more often than not
the world sets you against your own kind.
I wouldn't be surprised
if my sisters didn't speak to each other for the next twenty
    years.

I think that endless battle is every mother's greatest fear.
I know I miss them most
when I don't have to listen to them
whisper jeers about one another.
One of my sisters is an eternal child,
the other born another mother.

Black Tax Continued

Black tax is not so much a tax for being Black as it is a tax for not being white, as it applies to various other groups of POC in the same way it's my mom in the car, driving me to middle school and saying, you have to work twice as hard to get as far, and to be seen as half as good.

Black tax is never thinking you're beautiful, because the definition of beauty is blond hair and blue eyes, and even now, with the rise of the Kardashians, it's white women appropriating Black culture and features without the oppression.

Black tax is boys constantly telling you "you're not my type" because they don't want to say their type is white.

Black tax is having to be twice as beautiful to be half as loved.

Black tax is "you're just not right for the part" because the part needs to be someone gentle and innocent and your hips are too wide and your skin too dark and your lips too big, and "you don't fit into our vision."

Black tax is getting hired, only to be constantly told you were a diversity hire and don't deserve to be there.

Black tax is needing to code-switch and straighten your hair to be taken seriously. And then still not being taken seriously.

Black tax is entire communities of Black people growing up in ghettos that are remnants of Jim Crow and still being told there are no systems in place to keep them down.

Black tax is redlined school districts putting Black students in
worse schools.
Black tax is how the money follows the white children.
Black tax has its own IRS and it collects its debts
in the form of withholding social advancement.

Dear Black Girl

Over the course of your life bits and pieces of African American culture will become mainstream and our music will evolve and despite still being a part of our culture it will seem more and more like we were "losing" it. It will unsettle you how people can care so much for Black music and so little for Black people. For example, the Billboard Hot 100 charts were full of rap music in the same time frame where dozens of Black men were gunned down in the street. In mainstream non–African American communities it may become "cool" to be Black as long as you're not actually Black. You may come from R&B and soul food and the Southern Baptist church. They may try to take your cornrows and afros, without, of course, the living in constant fear that people hate us for things we can't control. Our culture has shaped this world. It will teach you to always check behind your back twice, we will teach you that your Black is beautiful, magnificent, people are constantly going to try and take it away from you, but just as they can never take your soul, they can never take *who you are.*

Wage Slavery

Will this body that
was just graced with the acrid
Taste of freedom be returned to
The slow burn of subservience?
Will my mother's mother's legacies
Be finger paintings in caves damned to
Never again see daylight
Might I just become
The flesh torn by a white man's teeth
More so than charcoal-grilled ribeye
Grinding on gold molars smolder over
High heat melting my fat for flavor
Like it wasn't woven to warm me.
Will strangers take the milk from my breast
And leave my children to go hungry?
Will this future turn on roasting spits
Like time often does
And take me back back back
To the fields

When I Stop Calling Mom, Mommy

Mommy became Momma
the first time I got catcalled.
Became Mom the first time my friend's father
leered at me and jeered are you sure
you wanna wear a dress like *that* around all these boys?
I swear.
Her nickname lost letters every time
the eyes that sliced across my body
were more hungry than adoring.
Mom became Ma
when a cop stopped me
from being tricked into sleeping with a senior
in the back seat of his car,
became Monette, just her name
when the same cop stopped to stare at my bare chest.
Mommy became "why didn't you save me"
when the days became a game of patiently waiting
for my body to be taken like hers was.

Black Tax Completed

The future in my prophecy is not forbidden
because these Black bodies pave the road to liberty
Because no one soul exists to be an enemy
because taxes strike fear in our society
but they go to build a better world in its entirety
I know that they don't see the way the system stacks
Our blood will pave that road and bones fill the cracks
No more hurt will happen here
Black tax.

Home

Pine needles and clean air
gust of tin-can gasoline
coffee and cinnamon
fried apples and bleach,
antique hiding
under a top layer of lemon Pledge.
The kitchen smells like olive oil,
pasta water, baking soda paste,

Amber, sandalwood,
and shea butter radiates

my brother is making toast.
the bread may be moldy.

Upstairs it reeks of teenagers and weed,
Bath & Body Works,
BO.
My room, like the boxes of Lush products.
Every Christmas—books. Paper.
covers every surface
has that . . . smell.
Old and new. It's everywhere.

When You Are Old Enough to Make Gumbo

1. The roux. You learn that if you leave the things you love to mull on their own over the fire they will burn. You take the flour and butter and your grandmother's cast iron and you whisk the paste every waking moment until it's brown like your skin. If you mess it up, wait two years, then try again.

2. Shrimp stock. Know that you can take the scraps of life and make masterpieces. If you have thrown away the shells, hope you haven't tossed away more important things, child, come back when you know the value of what you have.

3. Add the stock and shred the chicken, sausage, crab, let it simmer. Cook down, give it time, and it makes artwork. These are memories. These are your body.

4. When all is done, add the shrimp. At the very last moment. Heated by the aftermath of the stew, after Tony's and three color peppers chopped celery, heartbreak, know that if the shrimp goes in too soon it's gonna become rubber. Know you can't make gumbo before you're ready.

5. Know that rich flavor takes time.

To My Mother, Who I Caught Crying in the Shower

My mother had a mirror box.
She'd stand inside for hours and through the door I'd
    hear her cry.
She wouldn't let me go inside,
she'd never let me pry.
She said you'll never see the mirror box
until the day I die.
All women must know how
to silently cry.
When she dies
I'll find the key
to the room
she kept locked tight.
Sneak into infinity
one stupid silent night.
The mirror box is everything you've ever been
    before
the mirrors cover
every wall
and ceiling
and the floor.
You see your every angle
it's only you for miles.
You feel
the world's worst work of art. You see the ghost of all
    your trials.

I hate the mirror box
but I always return for more. My daughter hears my
    cries at night, my own internal holy war, when I die
    she gets the mirror box. Just like my mother, and hers
    before.

White, TN, Present

Stands for purity.
A child
a cloud
a soul.
Pale sin
and insecurity
all the colors
they say white
is whole.
Rock into dreams
or nightmares
coddled by white noise
I know
just who I'll find there.
Momma said
to stop it
with white boys.
She said
they don't want girls
like you
your spice
makes 'em scared.
She said everything
about their worlds
spites you
your struggle

is never shared.
They only crave curves
cased in alabaster skin.
They make you feel ugly.
I don't want you
to feel that pain again.
But damn
you always chasing
after them white boys.
And I don't know
what to do
I can tell you you're pretty
but they bruise
your soul black and blue.
They tell you you're strange
because they're afraid
to tell you the truth.
They're afraid
of themselves
the conformity of youth.
It's a powerful poison
they learn Black
is uncouth.
I don't know
how to show you
you're beautiful.
Your type is boys
who can't love you back.
She says

I don't know
how to tell you
you're beautiful.
Because you see beauty
in boys
who can't love your Black.

Girlhood Delights

Men, stretching at the blacktop revealing treasure trails and
    patches of underarm hair
Otis Redding.
Empty stretches of highway nineteen that breathe rust into
    the future.
Nibbling at the white centers of apples before choking down
    the bitter skin.
Boys with melanin.

The Blacktop

I cartwheel on the blacktop never stopping till I fall
Haunted by the ghost inside the hoops for basketball
Beyoncé blasts from speakers like Tina Turner before
And the mothers wag their fingers to the tempo on the floor
The grim delivery of an I love you not returned
The mothers shudder at the lessons they've all once learned
I crumple on the concrete dizzy mind like wasp abuzz
Sipping on a frosty drink and praying summer ends before
Formation does

Things That Are Annoying

The sting in your teeth after biting into sweet candy
Ovaries
Nostrils filled with pollen, sneezing more than twice in a row

Wasps shattering August skylines
Running
Praying
Running

"For a Black Girl," TN, 1970–Present

When you hear the words "for a Black girl"
you probably think of nothing at all . . .
because unless
you live the violence
that is suffering in silence
nothing wrong with those words
crosses your mind
because you can't see the boys
who ruined my birthday
by making monkey noises at us
to chase me out of their town.
I only ran the half mile
back to my house.
Their town was my town
but their curl pattern
don't cast no doubts
you can't see the hot combs
that rip away my ancestry
to make me the most European
I can be.
Because all I'll ever be to you
is a Black girl.
You think of Black excellence
I see Black oppression
you say I'm angry
I say sitting silent is a Black girl's first lesson

you say everything I do
is good "for a Black girl"
because you don't like that I'm smarter than you.
My people go to Harvard
you scream of affirmative action
we gotta be billionaires
to gain white traction
and I work my fingers to bone
on stubs of pencils
to say any word
that I don't want crowded out by my melanin.
And once my pigment
is tied to my paper
my first place becomes second
because I'm only good for a Black girl.
My momma was silver in every beauty pageant
because they refused to give gold
to someone with more color in their skin
than hatred in their heart.
And I lay out before you
like the corpses of my ancestors
the comebacks to all the comments
I let slide,

my skin is not made of caramel
no you cannot lick me
I'm not the monkey
if you're the one screeching like an ape
and telling me not to worry

if slavery comes back
because your family will buy me
gives me no comfort at all, jackass.
It gives me flashbacks to Black past
my ancestors' only allies were mules
they said we were genetically fools.
The fact that even the fiction of that
works out in your mind
shows you have no problem
viewing me as property.
The fact that you think putting me in chains
is kind, shows me
that you can't see my humanity.
The fact that 40 percent of sex-trafficking survivors are Black
is a statistic you've never heard
shows that society doesn't think my body belongs to me.
I'm pretty for a Black girl
And just because my soul isn't cased
in alabaster skin
you think you have the right
to take it for your own.
I'm pretty for a Black girl
because Black girls have Black kids
and white mommas don't see grandbabies
in niggers.
I'm pretty for a Black girl
because your internalized racism
lets you feel less bad
when we're on the wrong end of

triggers.
Gun-metal grey and dark days don't make change.
Bodies hang in loops and gangbangs the fruits strange.
Every day we wade through the KKK's meadow
and we know it never stops so we wait for dust to settle.
We breathe rhythm and poetry, and they still say it's ghetto.
All my people have hypoxia
from holding their breath
and waiting for the bullets to fly.
Our bodies lie in basements on the daily
but no newspapers plaster
if it's a Black girl baby.
Black kids don't get Amber Alerts
because nobody cares
if it's Latoya or Chiffon.
You think of nothing
when you say the phrase "for a Black girl"
because you don't see the crazy going on.
You call me Black girl into my thirties
because you don't think
I'll live long enough to be a woman.
You take your ignorance to the streets
because you don't see the storm that's coming.
I'm beautiful for any girl
and that's never gonna change
until the day you finally
get me back where you want me,
in chains.

Dying Town, Halls, TN

My momma played double Dutch
My momma was a beauty queen
My momma was a prodigy
My momma couldn't sit at lunch counters
She was born in the year 1970
The thing about small towns
Is they get stuck in time
I'm not sure Halls made
It past '59
(We're in Lauderdale County this time)
Small towns are like people who
Peak in high school
They never change
Because they're afraid of the fact
They are dying.
They just kick it in the '60s
Inside their own minds
In the confines of the
Frog Jump and Dyersburg lines
The stores never open
Only close
And if a new one comes around
It's gone by
First snows
I wonder
If it's healthy

To love a thing that's
As good as dead

My momma played double Dutch
My momma was a beauty queen
My momma was a prodigy
And the town that raised her up
Is becoming history

American Blessings, America, Present Day

I know a thing or two about American blessings
I know they are made for white men
I know in 1920 white women gained the right
To pretend things were =equal=
I know the American dream was done better in Canada

American blessings come in the form
Of the land of the free only speaking one language
In the form of believing we are free
In the form of thinking that free applies to everyone

America does not look like me
Only it does
Only one kind of person looks like an American blessing
That's why all the others come with qualifiers and prefixes

"I am a _____ American, and this place would rather I did not
    exist"
Fill in the blank with whatever
There is only one wrong answer
American blessings do not need papers
American blessings are ⅗ths of a person
American blessings

Seem like curses to the rest of us.

The Day My Grandmother Died, Halls, TN, February 17th, 2016

When the day comes
Let it nip at your bones like the bitter cold in the
     depths of Lake Superior
When the day comes let it
Take you
Swallowed by the fervid sea
Let your memories flash and dwindle
As the fire does
Let the embers hold kind words
Let them hold kisses
When the day comes to die
Don't fear the empty
Just wonder what it means to know
God
Wonder if it means to know God
And when your children say I love you
Into nothing
Pray your ghost answers.
When the day comes don't be
Startled
By your own phantom
When the day comes leave the red cross on the
     door

Leave your blessings in the will
Become at one with being still
Hope that when it comes
You don't fear that goodbye

Hair, Our Heads, Circa 2017

Infinite coils of constant majesty
pageantry and kryptonite
oceans of umber
that flow from my scalp
like tears flowed from the face of my grandmother when she
    lost hers to cancer
My hair
Bigger than my personality my muddled morality
and the hive-mind hatred for the oppressors of my people
all curled up in one
My hair is my identity a flash of solidarity for the silent 4C
    majority because it is the only way to express these feelings
without being the angry Black woman they want us to be
so they feel better
about the destruction of our civil liberty
and if they could take away my hair
my power
like my voice
you bet your ass they would
but they can't.
My hair
A pounding heart silken storybook
that hides my insecurities because they don't ask
about the scars
when they're saying
"oh my God your hair is so beautiful can I touch your hair"

and even when you say no,
they do it anyway
they don't realize that with every curl they squash
with their grubby little hands
they tear me away
from my history
strand by strand
and become a person
who took a stand
to tell us our styles were ghetto and unprofessional.
and I stand before you
with these words in my head surrounded by my hair
in a God-given halo
I beg of you to let me join the ranks of people
Who were not defined
by their skin
or their slang
or their free throw
or their
hair
but their words
let me be more
than the temple of tornadoes
that rise from my skull
let me be more
than braids or afro
because I am.
and let me speak
to my ancestors

through my halo
and tell them that
I have a voice.
I love my 3C
but I must let you know
that whether you're 4Z or 2B
any zig or zag or twist or turn
your curls may grow
you're bigger than your hair
speak up
shout out
and never be afraid
to grow

You Ain't Gotta Die and Go to Heaven or Hell to Get What You Deserve, Part II

The girl who bullied me and I were a lot alike like
I went to her birthdays alike
like we used to be friends alike
like we were both gay alike,
but the only difference was she was ashamed,
the thing shameful people hate most in the world
is those who love themselves

All my life I've been too loud
My momma was too loud
And hers before
And I've begun to wonder if my volume was ever really the
     problem.

A Question of Privilege, AP Human Geography, District 5, Nashville, TN, 2018

AP HUMAN GEOGRAPHY

Some people grow up believing that they deserve things
That they are owed
I once had a boy explain
To *me**
That he would be "affirmative actioned"
Out of a scholarship he deserved
Because his competition was a Black woman. When he won,
I wonder if he thought about how he lawyer-parented
And white-male-privileged that spot away from her.

He tells me "slavery was like two hundred years ago, man. Get
    over it."

I tell him our *country* is the same age.
That the maps we were studying are younger.

He calls me a stupid bitch. "It's not the same."
He swears that *those* two hundred years are
Important.

———

* Me: Black woman, could be perceived as a beneficiary of affirmative action.

Like it wasn't a simultaneous happening.
Like the men he idolized
Didn't devise empires on the history he dismisses.

I think . . .
If he saw me for sale in the marketplace,
On the corner of 3rd Ave, circa 1838*, he would buy me.
He doesn't ask permission now,
Why would he then?

I want to ask my teacher
Why I feel more when a white woman suffers.
If there's a historical explanation
I suppose it's because I'm conditioned to believe she is fragile
Meant to be cared for.

A Black woman is a workhorse
An old mare;†
As tough as the crisscross scars on her back since 1619‡
And the calluses that she can now barely feel—
The body defiled in ways that never heal

Lips:
That sputter blood like the empty promise of "one day."
It keeps spilling.

* The location of the largest slave market in Nashville, Tennessee
† A female horse, another word he doesn't think I know
‡ The year that whole slavery thing I need to get over started

—

We listen to Negro hymns in class during Black History
   Month.
That glory they sing of is only in the reach of death.

When we dies
We leaves behind childs to bear a white man's cross
And a family's curse of one day.

I sit in my AP Human Geography class and I wonder
If these people who think they deserve so much
Deserve salvation* too.

* ?

Rant, 2019, Nashville, TN

I'm sick of watching my people get slaughtered like
  animals.
I'm sick of having to tell my brother
he's not allowed to walk at the park because
he's too Black and too much of a man now
and I don't want to see his corpse plastered
all over the internet because he tried to go for a run.
I'm so tired of seeing these people being persecuted
under the presumption
that they're doing something wrong for existing
in a space that a white person doesn't think they should
  be in.
My heart is broken for all the Black mothers
who are burying their children.
My heart is broken that more Young Black men
die from this kind of violence than diabetes.
I'm heartbroken that people keep making excuses
for murderers because our society functions
on the presumption that white is right even when proven
  otherwise.
I'm tired of my heart being broken.
My grandfather died for a country that keeps killing his sons
  and it's not.
Fair.

It's not fair.
It's.
Not.

Right.

To Have a Name

I wonder if a mother's love
Can be found on the second X chromosome
If God built a womb as a portal from heaven's own
If Eve could have known
That womanhood was a power
That God never wanted to be revealed
But the forbidden fruit sewed
Eden into our DNA.

I wonder if Claudette Colvin knew
That something as simple as refusing to
Rise
Could incite something prophesied in Negro hymns for
    centuries
If she knew her revolutionary movement
Would live
In the shadow
Of Rosa Parks's memory
Black womanhood
Is being asked to bring gifts to parties you were never
    invited to
It's lighting everyone's candles with the fire alight in you
It's standing in solidarity with women who didn't fight for you
Because you know what oppression feels like
And I think that God just might

Love
Like Black women do.

My great-great-grandmother was enslaved
She took thoughts of freedom to her
Unmarked grave
Her daughter stood alongside
Sisters for rights that would
Never be hers in a lifetime
Revolution is
Imbedded in
My bloodline.
She couldn't have dreamed
What the next century brought in
The law,
In the hands of justice Jane Bolin
The first judge
In this country to be a
Black woman.
Changing a future she would never see.
Every
Vote we cast
Should honor her memory

Cast that ballot like that candle burning with
Ancestral flame
It is the legacy they fought for
Let them see what became

Of the children
Of the country

Of the women

Who got the chance
To have a name
If words are bullets then your ballot is a
Semi-
Auto-
Matic
It's the way your voice can shoot through the
Silence
And
The
Static
If the sealing of your lips is far more
Than
Syste-
Matic
Look back
At all the mothers who wielded their weapons for you.
This holiday is an empty promise if we don't use it
To see there's more to our mission
Look at Atlanta's lines
Voting booths with locked-shut doors
By governors with flimsy spines
My people who can't vote for
Nonviolent crimes committed back in '99,

—

I

Watch my sister's best friends go to prison.

I watch the boys I saw become
Men
Become felons and lose every right
Our ancestors fought for.

I see pictures of today's suppressed voters in black and white
So people still think this is
History.

It's not my tomorrow I'm fighting for
It's my daughter's
I'll stand guard at her door
As Grandma waded in the waters
Every vote is hope that no more of my blood
Will lie in unmarked graves.
It's the hope that my babies will always be called
By their names

Burn your textbooks
if they tell you there's nothing
More to change.

—

Women the world has tried to silence are women who
Know what needs repair
Shirley Chisholm said if they don't give you a seat,
Bring.
A.
Folding.
Chair.
For Black women,
This privilege has not been here for one hundred years
But when it comes to revolution ask Eartha, Angela,
We have always been
The pioneers
The love

My great-great-grandmother held for me from pasts afar
Was strong
Because it drew its power from and burned just like
The nearest star.

From Malala
To Assata
From the classroom
To the polls
Womanhood and the sun's fire
Reside
Inside
Our souls
That through every election
And the world we change in kind

The garden in our bodies
Will find solace in our minds
And the waters that we waded in
Bring joy in gentler times.

That my daughter
Has the future Eve
And every other mother dreams
That Eden
Will be
Home again
And America
Will be

Redeemed.

The Untouchable

I pan for names like gold.
This history I have spent so long searching for
Is not the kind to be found in books
Not the kind to make nice with cameras
It's a phantom
I don't know how I've managed
to love nameless women so dearly,
yet every night I pray
that they look down on me with pride.
And as my hands grow older and rougher
I wonder if they will ever have the same sensation
as my forgotten history.

Bad Dreams, After the Death of George Floyd, 2020

I take in air like a head shot
Ma says to breathe don't get caught
Sometimes it burns call it hot box
They want me to choke that's black rot
Oxygen's not toxic
We live in fear if we want it
She tells me stay alive stay alive
Lived nightmares many times
And I think I'm hooked on bad memories
Pains like the kiss from old enemies
Breathe too much blood is the penalty
The Judas kiss is your specialty
Why do my mothers lay in unmarked graves?
Our life force is soil seeded by slaves
They say it's a privilege living in this place
We just survive and die might be a white one
Snort coke in the back seats of windowless jeeps
If they gun down a brother that's all in good fun
Don't care 'bout the blood if it stays in the hood son

And I been having bad dreams
I've been having bad dreams
The news telling me bad things
Maybe it's just bad dreams

—

And sad, taste like a curse word
Mad cuz the cops can hurt them now
They get standing ovations for killing us.
And once the show's over they'll be billing us
For all the buzz we stole from the Hadids and Jenners
Why does it matter if our murdered men were sinners
And I'm watching pigs popping off tear gas in the crowd and
I am way more than ⅗ths pissed off right now
My Ma says we're fighting a four-hundred-year war
Don't wanna say sorry for my Blackness no more
Learned 'bout the Black codes since the dawn of your time
One. Don't commit two crimes at the same time!
And you know being Black counts as one crime
Apathy kills more Black people than hate
At this rate eons of pain feels like fate
In a world that sees Black sins when it's just Black skins
When Black men start dying nothing ever happens

And I been having bad dreams
I've been having bad dreams
The news telling me bad things
Maybe it's just bad dreams

Oh I been having bad dreams

Climbing Out Windows

Both my grandmother
and my sister have a propensity for climbing out of windows.
They are very much alike,
the high yellow kind
that likes to live on the wild side,
you might call them bad kids.
I say they're braver than I could ever be.
My sister is reckless in every facet of her life,
including optimism.
She's recklessly kind.
Recklessly compassionate.
Recklessly optimistic.
I am terrified she will die younger than my grandmother did.
She is the fire that I
in my overabundance of caution
would be lost without.

Athena & Ida

Ever since I was little, I hated gym class
whether it's playing the same games
pacer test that gives whiplash
perhaps it's just that I hate the monotony
of walking back and forth.
It's the labor of change without progress.
I think this day and age our laws are much the same
we're changing street names
instead of changing games
but you see Nashville is a battleground
much like the ones found in Athens
where maidens made their own battalions.
Lysistrata-like women showing what happens
when mothers have a mission
when Harry Burn had to be a good boy
and feed into the vision.

This city's streets are a temple
to the infinite wisdom of those who seek progress more than
    change.
Of those who stood dauntless even restrained.
Of those who know love often means walking into battle.
Of those who know there are no kisses in the dark times.
In the old days maybe love served as a shield
from feeling wars waged but here
there are only your own bones.

We now stand as the linchpin of a moment in history
where in isolation we must know we are not alone.
Alone is a notion that changes with time
whether it's crowded and hopeless or solitary confined
but I'm starting to realize
that there is no such thing as true solitude in Nashville.
We stand in tandem with the history held in this very land.
And if we made it through the battles
at the top of every last hill
we can survive the fight for progress again.

Have you ever stood beneath the stone pillars
in the great lake of green
watching the sky becoming twilight sewn
in shades you've never seen
the strings of fate weave through the heavens
when the night goddess's moon first gleams
and in that moment you are infinite. Timeless.

This mythos is carved of marble stone
yet lives in temples of flesh and bone
this altar, to the goddess known as Athena.
Athens itself stood as a monument
to the goddess of war
the armored protector it's said that Zeus bore.
Through centuries it stood
through battles and through peacetimes.
When women become warriors, battles end swiftly.

Nowhere is this more well-known than here in Music City.
No one knows it as well as Ms. Ida B. Wells
and frankly, Frankie knows it too.
A hundred years ago we were halfway through the battle.
And those who stand here with me
the rest is now up to you.
The laws we made have climbed
on the women left behind but for the first time
we are trying to lift each other.
And when our battle cries take the tunes of lullabies
you'll see that nobody knows combat like a mother.

As I write this I have eight months and twenty-three days
    before I'm old enough to vote in this country
I've got negative seventeen years three months and seven days
since your votes began affecting me.
They say the meek shall inherit the earth,
but they inherit the laws and the wrongs as well.
The children are left when all is done
to rebuild the empires that fell.
We the people must contend that
there are laws we must amend
even when those in power try to bend and break us.
But when resolves start to shake we must resolve to stay
    awake
because the things that tear us down are what awake us.
The Parthenon in its spires to the peak of its crown
is a phantom standing over you, its legacy looking down.
When the odds are against us we work best. Just watch.

We don't need to fill the shoes of phantoms to walk. In
    tandem
we won't stop until progress is here and it's now.
Cigarette ash and shellac of the past
turn back to coal to power streetlamps that stand as sacrificial
    fires,
smog, and smoke signals,
a reminder of the hallowed ground we walk in kind,
Ida and Frankie like the huntress god born of Zeus's mind
unashamed and unbroken.

Cannibalism, Present Day, Tennessee

My grandfather died for the country that keeps killing his sons
    and it's not fair
I don't think he can breathe in that casket and it's not fair
He left behind a daughter for a country that hates her and it's
    not fair
I'm sick to my stomach all the time now
I suppose when they used to kill my mothers
and fathers it was like killing expensive cattle
I don't think they were cannibals so
When they watched them bleed out to water
the crops it may have been just to get that rush of power
Or maybe they were using flesh and bone to ensure fertile soil.
That blood doesn't do much good watering concrete
watering sidewalks
and pavement
and the carpets in our own houses
And I think it's a war on two fronts
If I'm not mowed down in a numbers game in the classroom
It's a power play by my neighbors, I wonder
What it feels like to be safe?
I think they kill Black men because they can't buy Black
    women to rape anymore.
Is it a craving to defile the sanctity of Black bodies?
Maybe it is cannibalism

Convocation

I wrote a poem, every year of my education
Twelve years of evolving into the artist you see before you
A strange girl on the spectrum who wrote songs during
Her lessons and read books in place of making sense
Of numbers
My best friends have all been teachers
I pencil every poem for Ms. Robinson
For Dr. Anderson I dot every i
And after all this time writing for those who taught and cared
   for me
I'm learning the real weight of a goodbye
If I could write a love poem to a time gone by
I am the ship of Theseus
I am a different I than the one who wrote a poem

On fourth-grade graduation
To tell my favorite teachers I'd find them all again one day
That I would be one of them one day and I mean it
I am not just my mother's daughter
I am of metro public schools
For every broken heart and late paper
Educators gave me the tools
And I promise to the heavens
I will never truly say goodbye
Due to one of my favorite classroom rules

People may not remember what you said,
But they will always remember how you made them
    feel.
I will follow in Dr. Kenyae Reese's stead
And help another generation of children heal.

The Chosen People, TN, Always

I think they may be afraid of where
The Bible takes place
That God's chosen people
Were darker than dark white
They might be afraid
Of a Black man preaching peace
Because they are known to
Throw the first stone even
When they are sinners
The Bible gave them lessons
But they don't take advice
From coloreds and the
Son of God could never be
A nigger because Christ was
Above all and pride only cometh
Before the fall when it
Is slaves claiming their own names
I mean their roots
Much like Egyptian chains
Are built from wrought iron
They are rusted and rotted
And only left
To choke the chosen people

Black Mothers, TN

Black women have
Black babies who become Black women who have Black
    babies
And they are all dying
I spend most of my time trying to reconcile the fact that I am
    no longer a Black baby
I am well on my way to being a Black
Mother
My great-grandma was one twice over by the time she was
    my age
I am afraid to watch my children suffer
How am I supposed to tell my sons
That they are wanted men
When they are infants
These false pharaohs want me to drown them
I think that they will be very likely dead by the time they get to
    high school

Black women have Black babies who become Black boys who
    become corpses before they are men or fathers

My Black daughters will be women far too soon
When they are still gentle
Men will say to them that they are
Unyielding
I pray they don't understand the words

That they never know the feeling
That they are invisible to leather hands
Like they are to the rest of the world

White men have Black children and those children only know
    they are bastards
I won't say it out loud but I hope that if I bear a white man's
    child they will have their father's eyes and privileges
I wonder what it means to gentrify my own womb
People tell me I am already gentrified

Black fathers have Black sons and go to prison when fathers
    stay we wonder if they are broken

We are all broken
On my family tree I found two slaves.
One could be seen because she was freed early
One was left by name in a will
Both of these women had daughters marked in the census as
    mulattos
Both of these women were labeled as widows
When Black mothers are raped by slave owners
They have children who could expose secrets big enough that
    they are gifted freedom

Black women have Black babies who become Black women
    and Black men and it does not take much black to be in
    danger.

When We Realized We Were Black

You don't see color until you're made to feel it.
When white girls on the bus know you as
Negro, but not your name.
When teachers threaten to beat your Black ass
Or you're the only Black girl in class and the only one not
    invited
When you are not a primary color
When the schools are first integrated
But the streets are still segregated
When you see a man gunned down for the first time
When you sell a little boy a pencil and he says don't talk to me
    nigger
When your best friend calls your hair nappy
When you move back to the South.
10 years old
5 years old
9 years old
The day you were old enough to read the colored signs.

A Thousand Generations

Towns die but legacies are forever
History is climate more than weather
Will I love another place so much?
Never
Because even when we're apart Halls means
    together
In my mother's other home
I am the bearer of this prophecy
From the moment
Her body opened
We,
My sisters and me,
Were destined to be the
Someday
They've been waiting on
For centuries.
We are
The culmination of a thousand generations
Of brilliant women
Of real prayers
Of internal warfare, long, long deferred dreams
Look at every voice
And every poem that graced a page
That has now somehow

Found its way to your eyes.
I hope
When you look at me
You see them.

I'm Still Walking

I miss the days before the world started dying. I miss when we were all young enough that we could all get together in the summers. Times where all of us were *actually* together, all passing stories around like the box of pizza from Exxon, because after all a story is only as much as the last person who loves it. My mom tells me remembering lineage and breaking generational curses is the most important thing you can do in your lifetime. She tells me generational curses are American curses. I'm hoping that by owning up to their mistakes I may be spared from them. But in the words of Yvonne, "Keep living. Don't ever say what you're never gonna do." So I'll live some more and make some bad choices, and I'll suck the marrow from chicken bones. And everywhere in this world I walk, I'll walk with Gentry. Because this is my legacy. These are the wars we have always been crafted in the fire of. This battle between the world and girlhood may never end, but I hope I have given you some weapons to keep fighting because no matter how often girlhood dies, no matter how often the world tries to kill it, on the blacktop in the little town of Halls there will always be girls finding their way home, even if Gentry won't be there beside them.

ACKNOWLEDGMENTS

My mom always tells me that faith the size of a mustard seed
can move mountains
    And so, I want to take the time to thank the grains of faith
that I have counted
    The people whose belief in me and Gentry has amounted
Into the book you see before you
    I want to thank my parents for always being there
    I want to thank Briana Burtsell for all her love and care
    I want to thank Dr. Learotha Williams for being my histori-
cal eyes
    I want to thank the Lacys and Springfields for helping me to
rise
    I want to thank the staff of Hillsboro High School
    And the Tennessee Young Writers' Workshop
    And my aunt Jacqui Springfield; though she's gone, my love
for her won't stop
    My amazing agent, Lauren MacLeod

And my editors, David and Darryl
The Rachels, Rokicki and Kind
Cassie Gonzales for jacket design
Andy Ward and Avideh Bashirrad
Toby Ernst and Emily Hotaling
Allan Spencer and Loren Noveck
All of your praises I have to sing
Julie Cepler and all the family who didn't fit on this little tree
For everyone who aided and guided me
Denise Cronin and Benjamin Dreyer
Thank you all for your passion and fire
I couldn't have done this alone
Thank you for helping me walk Gentry home

ABOUT THE AUTHOR

ALORA YOUNG is a college student, an actor, and the Youth Poet Laureate of the Southern United States. Her poetry has appeared in *The New York Times* and *The Washington Post,* and she has performed her poetry on CNN, CBS, and the TEDx stage. Alora currently attends Swarthmore College.

Twitter: @Alora_young
Instagram: @aloraofficielle

ABOUT THE TYPE

This book was set in Albertina, a type-face created by Dutch calligrapher and designer Chris Brand (1921–98). Brand's original drawings, based on calligraphic principles, were modified considerably to conform to the technological limitations of typesetting in the early 1960s. The development of digital technology later allowed Frank E. Blokland (b. 1959) of the Dutch Type Library to restore the typeface to its creator's original intentions.